LOVE, VIRTUES
AND COMMANDMENTS
AN INTERFAITH PERSPECTIVE

SAJJAD S. HAIDER, PhD

FOREWORD BY
SEYYED HOSSEIN NASR

ABC INTERNATIONAL GROUP, INC.

Library of Congresss Cataloging in Publication Data

Haider, Sajjad S.
    Love, Virtues and Commandments: An Interfaith
    Perspective

    Includes bibliographical references.
    1. Interfaith. 2. Religions. I. Haider, Sajjad. II. Title.
    BL53.U45 200'.1975.16302
ISBN: 0-934905-79-7

Illustrations by Khalida Rahman and Maliha Haider

PUBLISHED BY
ABC INTERNATIONAL GROUP, INC.

DISTRIBUTED BY
KAZI PUBLICATIONS
3023 W. BELMONT AVENUE
CHICAGO IL 60618
(T) 773-267-7001; (F) 773-267-7002
EMAIL: KAZIBOOKS@KAZI.ORG

To my dear son,
Qasim A. Haider,
and my youngest grandson,
Zahid Sajjad Ali,
my youngest granddaughter,
Noorina Fatima Ali and
my great-grandson, Reza Ali Haider,
all my children and grandchildren, nephews and nieces,
their peers groups
with prayers.

May Almighty One God guide them on
the glorious path of righteousness, with
love and altruism for humanity, beyond
the boundaries demarked by man-made labels
of different religions and sects.

CONTENTS

FOREWORD

In a world torn by strife on all levels from the physical and economic to the intellectual and spiritual, any attempt to bring out the voice of the unanimous tradition of wisdom which shines within and through the diverse religions and wisdom traditions of the world is a most laudable task. The Quranic dictum, *"Verily to every people a messenger has been sent,"* is a clear scriptural confirmation of this truth that God has left no human collectivity without a truth of Divine Origin and this universal manifestation of the truth can still be found everywhere despite veils which have covered to various degrees the original pristine message in many climes. There is a universal doctrine of which various religions are so many confirmations, that doctrine being the Unity of the Divine Principle with all that such a doctrine implies metaphysically and practically. And it is only in the confirmation of this sacred truth, while respecting the particularities of each sacred world, particularities which have issued from the Origin itself, that there is the possibility of veritable discourse and mutual understanding between various peoples. This dialogue means of course discourse between various forms of truth and not truth and error for the claims of truth cannot be compromised for any end even peace among men. The calling of the truth remains the highest call and it is only on the basis of truth that serious accord can be created. Without it all peace is a fake peace as the history of the modern world, so much of it based not on perennial truths but their negation, demonstrates so amply.

It is to the credit of this book to bring out some of these truths as they pertain to various aspects of human life by going back to the original sources of wisdom in various religions of the world. The references quoted by the author, with a few exceptions, are to those texts most revered by followers of various religions. By appealing to such sacred texts and inspired writings of figures revered as spiritual authorities in each religion, the author is able to move beyond theological and philosophical disputations to the bedrock of various faith systems wherein is to be found in a most evident way the universal truth spoken in different dialects of the Spirit.

Needless to say, there are religions which form a family and have closer affinities among themselves than they do with numbers of other families of religions. Examples could be given of Abrahamic, Indian, Iranian or Shamanic families of religions wherein one can find concrete examples of the principle just cited. Coming from an Islamic background, the author naturally pays greater attention to the Abrahamic family, consisting of Judaism, Christianity and Islam and provides detailed comparative parallels between the Old Testament, the New Testament and the Quran. But he does not confine his vision to this world. Coming as he does from the Indian subcontinent, he also provides textual testimony from Indian religions and even those of the Far East and demonstrates the global character of the teachings discussed in various chapters.

The suffering experienced by the author during his youth at the time of the partition of India is reflected through the pages of this book. It must be especially painful to him to see the state of Hindu Muslim relations in that land a half a century later. He therefore pleads for the putting aside of human differences in order to reach accord among people on the human level. It must be asserted, however, that religious accord is not possible in the human atmosphere but only in the "Divine Atmosphere" to quote Frithjof Schuon who has spoken so eloquently of the "transcendent unity of religions." Nor can the human state with its imperfections be ignored or abolished as if it did not exist. But the reality of this "transcendent unity" can be brought out and an intellectual "elite" created who can understanding this harmony in the "the Divine Stratosphere" and contribute to creating better mutual understanding among peoples even if not everyone is capable of comprehending that unity which transcends all forms.

The present book is a valiant effort in this direction motivated by love and concern, even if at times the author allows sentimental elements to ignore difficult human realities which are nevertheless present and must be taken fully into consideration. It is our hope that this book will be read by those of good will who wish to gain greater understanding of other peoples and also want to realize more fully how the perennial wisdom embedded in various traditions concern and are applicable to our lives today as they were to the lives of those who lived yesterday and will live tomorrow. A work born of understanding and love cannot but affect the minds and hearts of those who earnestly seek understanding combined with that all pervading love and sympathy to which the Persian poet Rumi was alluding when he said, "The Prophet came to bring forth mutual sympathy [in the original Latin sense of *sym-pathia*]."

Seyyed Hossein Nasr
March, 1997

PREFACE

Every thing in heaven and earth, the smallest atom with its invisible constellation, the cosmic spread of far and near galaxies, all the elements, and fauna and flora on this planet, are governed by the laws of the One God, the most intelligent Creator. The whole universe has accepted the unshared sovereignty of God by following these laws. The acceptance of His laws by the physical universe is its created nature. Human beings are offered this possibility of obedience as divine mercy and as attribution of His justice. But this submission to His divine guidance has to be adopted by choice and with the free will of human beings. The One God, His universal love, laws of guidance and similar needs of human minds and souls are facets of reality for the peace, health and harmony of a human society. It is logically evident that His divine guidance should be the same for every human society and every nation, conveyed to them in their own languages through His messengers at various periods in history on an extended scale of time.

Its universality, therefore, should be acknowledged by the human race to avoid conflicts. A few quotations from The Holy scriptures substantiate this divine reality.

We sent not a messenger except (to teach) in the language of his (own) people, in order to make (things) clear to them [14:4].

Every messenger has conveyed one and the same message.

Not a messenger did We send before you (O Muhammad) without this inspiration sent by Us to him: that there is no God but I; therefore, worship

ix

(obey) and serve Me [23:25].

> *We sent Noah to his people: He said, "O my people! worship (obey) God! You have no other God but Him. Will you not fear Him?' [23:23].*

> *Abraham behold, he said to his people, 'Obey God and fear Him that will be best for you—if you understand' [39:16].*

Prophet Moses said to his people,

> *Know therefore, that the Lord your God, He is God, the faithful God who keeps covenant and mercy with them that love Him and keep His commandments to a thousand generations. You shall, therefore, keep the commandment, and the statutes, and the ordinances which I command you this today, to do them [Deut. 7:9,11].*

Prophet Jesus conveyed God's message to his people,

> *For God, He is my God and your God: So obey Him: This is a straight way [43:64].*

> *We ought to obey God rather than men [Acts 5:29].*

Prophet Muhammad said to human beings, as directed by God,

> *O people, adore and obey your Guardian God, Who created you and those who came before you, that you may have the chance to learn righteousness [2:21].*

Thus God's living religion has remained the same in spirit, reality, constitution and essential quality. The sources of unity and universality are the revelations from the One God at various times. The formation of sects with various labels is against the very essence and principles of preaching the divine message delivered by His messengers for peace, love and unity. It is a universal truth, supported and fostered by logic, that "Your will be done," is the only straight path to human salvation and ascension to His kingdom. The universality of the divine message is the greatest blessing of God, showered on the parched mind and soul of mankind. The aim is to cultivate the moral landscape of human existence on this earth.

The agony of human hypocrisy in response to the divine message in history has flayed the sides of humanity exposing blood stained scars. The prevailing traits of animality in human beings, self-centeredness, and amoral intelligence, have found a hundred and one excuses to hate, harm, and exploit other human beings. The biggest excuse, unfortunately, is self-made differences in faith, religion and even different interpretations of the same divine messages. Hans Kung, the world-renowned theologian, points out in his book, *Christianity and World Religions*[1] that the most fanatical, the cruelest political struggles are those that have been colored, inspired, and legitimized by religion. He presented the solution to this malady, "No world peace without religious peace."

Human beings, bestowed with numerous gifts claiming superiority over other creatures have disappointed the One God's messengers by misusing the gift of freedom to make the choice between 'right' and 'wrong.' The majority of human beings have followed the pride and prejudice of racial superiority, self made religious supremacy, pseudo intellectual-excellence, martial preponderance, physical advantages and manipulation of resources. The ruling masters have created unthinkable miseries and sufferings for their servants. The recorded incidences of man's cruelty to man in the twentieth century have marred the face of humanity.

In 1947, British India was drenched in human blood as freedom was being sought through the division of the subcontinent. Tyranny and cruelty reigned in every sphere of human life which regressed to the lowest level of animality. Over a million innocent people were massacred including women and children, young and old. There were no gas chambers but enough kerosene oil to burn houses with residents locked inside. There were no guns but enough clubs, swords and hatchets to smash, cut and chop life, the gift of God, into pieces and pulp. It was a sport to throw children in the air and to catch them at the point of the spear in front of their parents. The most heinous, grossly wicked and most cruel treatment of a human by another human was in the name of two religions. One believed and preached non-violence and the other moralized the teachings with love and peace. This was happening before my eyes and I could do nothing except to internalize and interlace in my soul the sharp pain, piercing grief, and intense afflictions of human tragedy.

Even today the atrocities of human beings toward other humans on a mass scale, are broadcasted, televised and printed by the media.

How can we forget the heinous crimes of the holocaust in Germany during Hitler's regime; the catastrophe and bloodbath in India and Pakistan at the time of partition; the devastation and destruction showered on human life in the name of the communist revolution in Russia and China; the ethnic cleansing in Bosnia, streams of human blood drowning the dignity of humanity in Somalia, Rowanda, Afghanistan and Zaire; agony and human sufferings by the death of millions in the Iran-Iraq War between two armies following the same religion; atrocities and lack of trust destroying efforts of peace in the Middle East. All this and other inhumanity, wickedness and barbarity of one person to another in the name of religion, skin color, racial pride, vainglory of wealth and self glorification of command over weapons of destruction, have snatched away peace and contentment from sensitive souls. The deep valleys in the human soul are filled with dreadful apprehension, burning grief, distressful depression, weeping afflictions, discouragements and pricking hopelessness. Hardly a week goes by when we do not hear of bloodbaths in various parts of the world. The murders of innocent people by terrorists in the name of some cults and self assumed religious rights have defaced any claim of righteousness. It is cruelty and fraud camouflaged by their faith.

Poverty may be entangling life with pestiferous tentacles in slums in the heart of most affluent and resourceful nations; or its tempest, roaring high, may cover the whole nation except the palaces of the dictatorial government and mansions of friends and family of the governing party installed by the self-serving power of some foreign government. The corruptible power, on the other hand, in full command of advanced technology and means of mass destruction, manipulates and exploits the world in the interests of its economic supremacy and continuance of super-power status. I fear that, if the struggle to develop and acquire better and better weapons of mass-destruction is continued by every nation, the day is not far off when the life giving light of the sun will be covered with dark clouds of ashes after burning the fauna and flora on this globe.

What worries a sensitive soul is the fast progressing resourcefulness for mass destruction. Geographical distances are shrinking fast. A country thousands of miles apart on the map seems next door due to the advancement in the delivery system. The stock piles of biological weaponry and availability of lethal nerve gas components at the command of tyrant governments can inflict unbearable torture and the mass murder of innocent people.

The moral picture of the human race at present is also deplorable.

The studies, statistics, reports, talk shows, and TV programs referred to in various speeches and reports are full of grief. The moaning and mourning is becoming an awakening. One can hear the indictments, however hushed: "The world has lost its sense of moral values. This moral bankruptcy will lead to a criminal society. It can be so completely de-moralized as to be unable to differentiate between right and wrong. The hunger for technology and greed have obsessed the mind, robbing it of the ability of moral discrimination."[2]

The reports about the developing world are in no way better than those of the developed world. The moral fabric has been shredded into pieces by the cruel hands of greed, corruption, ethnic hatred, national pride, and self assumed religious superiority of their sects. Every effort is being made to find reasons to create differences and justify human cruelty. Within the limited resources and restricted sphere of action, they jump on each other's throat. Fatalistic attitudes prevail amongst the illiterate masses that extinguish any flame of hope.

Hatred is chocking the spiritual life of humanity. The all-embracing religious strivers have to recognize the anguish of the pestilence-stricken world. Love, only, blessed with the divinity of the universal message, can provide the healing balm to badgered souls.

There has never been so much distrust, distress, affliction, and terror. The history of the 20th century is stunned to see the earth soaked with human blood. The dingy dilemma is that the spirit of Cain is howling high to squelch the spirit of Abel. How did this happen? Who is responsible? Who has spurned the spiritual wisdom, the divine gift. The answer is clear and shining like the sunlight in the universality of the divine message. Prophet Malachi of Israel answered by asking:

> Have we not all one father?
> Has not One God created us?
> Why do we deal treacherously every
> man against his brother,
> Profaning the covenant of our fathers?
> (Malachi 2: 10 in the Old Testament).

Only through the acceptance of the universality of divine love, grace and justice, can human beings prevent themselves from the harmful effects of selfishness, greed and hatred.

*****

Efforts are being made through this work to draw your attention towards the universality of the divine message of God that is for all human race. The Absolute Truth demands a firm faith and belief in the One God, in His angels, in all His Holy Books (the universality of His message), and in all His messengers without discrimination.

God is not interested in rituals.

> *Has the Lord a great delight in burn-offerings and sacrifices, in harking to the voice (command) of the Lord? Behold, to obey is better than sacrifice, and to hearken than the fat of rams* (First Samuel 15: 22).

> *It is not their meat nor their blood that reaches God: it is your piety (obedience) that reaches him* [22:37].

The divine message emphasizes embracing the Truth and doing right even if no worldly advantage can be ascertained immediately.

Rabindra Nath Tagore said, "Every newborn child brings a message that the Creator is still hopeful of human race." His divine revelation ennobles the newborn child with consciousness to distinguish between right and wrong when he/she develops faculties of making choice.

> *His Mercy is upon all His works* (Psalms 145:9).

> *He makes His sun rise on the evil and on the good, and sends rain on the just and on the unjust* (Matthew 5:45).

> *Our Lord! Your reach is over all things in mercy and knowledge* [40:7].

In addition to the above realities: the universality of God's divine message and deplorable responses to the divine message from the majority of the human race, there is a third reality aiming at reclaiming human dignity. There are conscientious energies being generated in a segment of human society awakening the masses to change their path that is otherwise leading them to moral destruction. Mine is a humble offering to this third reality.

Human beings are not made perfect. The only exceptions are His messengers and other models of submission to His Will. Thus, sinners have every chance of repentance and forgiveness. His mercy, forgiveness, and grace over the human race are the embodiments of His attributes. The moment a sinner, in the name of his/her saviour repents, begs for mercy and strives to stay on the straight path, His Mercy breaks through turning the dark corridors of gloom into bright shinning chambers lit with His love and grace. He is the Creator of every human being irrespective of the race, color, and creed. Faith in Him is not expressed in words. It is expressed through deeds in obedience to His commandment. We are what we do and while our faith shapes our deeds they in turn foster and nourish our faith.

> The greatest enemies of God are those who profess His religion and do acts of infidelity (Saying of Prophet Muhammad).

Prophet Jesus said,

> *By works a man is justified and not by faith only"* (James 2:24).

> *Let us not love in word, neither in tongue but in deed* (I John 3:18).

> *Why call you me, Lord, Lord, and do not the things which I say* (Luke 6:46)?

All the prophets, sages and seers have emphasized the importance of faith substantiated by deeds as the commanding spirit of the divine message:

> To see what is right and not to do it is a want of courage (Confucius).

> To preach religion and not to practice it is to be like a parrot saying a prayer (Buddha).

> The thoughtless man, even if he can recite a large portion of the law, but is not a doer of it, has no share in religious life, but is like a cowherd counting the cows of others (Buddha).

There is a great emphasis in His commandments to love other human beings and do virtuous acts resulting in welfare of human society.

Prophet Jesus said,

> *You shall love the Lord your God with all your heart, with all your soul, and with all your mind.*
>
> *You shall love your neighbor as your-self.*
> (Matthew 22:37, 39).

> Shall I not inform you a better act than fasting, alms, and prayers? Making peace between one another because enmity and malice tear up heavenly rewards by the roots (Saying of Prophet Muhammad).

Callousness towards feelings and needs of other human beings is gross negligence, heedlessness and indifference which are negative attitudes and, in fact, disobedience to His will. On the other hand, all those human acts that fall under the category of being honorable and are known for their beneficial effects are considered upright, worthy, and righteous, under His will. They elevate one individual or one society over another in the measures and criteria of God's religion. Such acts add the dimension of value to life. They heighten the fidelity of the soul and embellish the personality and render it endearing and beautiful. Rays of hope spring out of the confused, smoggy, smirching and smoldering mind, directing human beings to do the best they can to remember the unity, commonality and universality of the One God's religion.

*****

I have not attempted to compare one faith (religion) with another, or to judge and arrange them in order of merit. The labels of these religions are man-made just to create differences, to look for excuses to hate each other in defiance of the Absolute and Truthful message of love for fellow human beings and all His creatures. Only faith in the One God, submission, subservience and obedience to His will and commandments is a solid guarantee for 'peace' (*islam* in Arabic).

I have not the slightest intention of offering a new dogma nor any desire to market a magic fix for the ills of humanity. I only affirm the essence of all His existing revelations. I do believe that any person, irrespective of carrying any label, can achieve peace by believing in One sovereign God, His angels, all His books, all His messengers and foster his/her belief with the deeds which are commanded (you shall and you shall not) by the One God. Those commands under divine love have had universal value throughout the history of mankind. These are supported by rationality and aim at the spiritual health and physical welfare of human society.

I would encourage the followers of their respective man-made-religious and sectarian-labels to honor the jurisprudence of their religion's authorities on the interpretation of laws, (examples: marriage, inheritance, rituals, restrictions on food, etc. etc.) and to acquire spiritual peace they have to believe in worshiping One God and follow this by the deeds of His fundamental commandments ("you shall" and "you shall not").

I do not claim to have included anything new in this book. I am conscious of my limitations. Therefore, a humble effort has been made to draw attention towards the basics of the Creator's universal and divine love and laws of guidance which have never changed in the journey of mankind over time. The only way human beings can defeat satan and obliterate the hatred for each other from human minds is to follow His commandments by faith and deeds. Let us not pay attention to labels of various religions and sects. Let us embrace each other with love, care and compassion because our needs are the same and the prescriptions of salvation and ascension to His kingdom are the same in every religion. The differences are man-made. I would like to end this preface with a prayer from Guru Nanak: "By your grace, may every one be blessed with peace in the world."

Sajjad Haider

ACKNOWLEDGMENTS

Human language has never been able to express the deep feelings of gratitude that human beings felt towards the most Merciful and Compassionate Creator. I am fully aware of my ineptitude and insufficiency in saying, "Thank You, O Almighty God." These deep and profound feelings of gratefulness blooming in every corner of my heart and soul cannot be expressed in words.

The human race should acknowledge prophethood with deep respect and gratitude towards God who sent them to deliver His message to human beings in the respective language of every nation. I bow my head offering deepest regards, reverence, devotion and praise to every holy messenger and prophet of God (peace, blessing and salutation be on all of them.). My acknowledgments with respectful admiration are humbly submitted to the following messengers of God, as a special tribute.

1. Prophet Noah: the builder-captain of Noah's Ark and progenitor of human beings and other forms of animal life after navigating in the great flood under the command of God.

2. Prophet Abraham: one of the most devoted servants and a true friend of God, a chosen messenger, symbol and model of the divine message, father of the ancestry of exalted prophets and messengers.

3. Prophet Moses: one of the most distinguished givers of the divine law of God, having the exceptional honor of direct conversation with 'HUWA,' the Creator of heaven and earth.

4. Prophet Jesus: born of the Holy Virgin Mary, who was chosen by God above the women of all nations. He is distinguished as Word and Spirit of God. He is a personification of the Creator's love, compassion and mercy for human beings. His special assignment is to give eternal life to the dead and cure ailments of body, soul and mind. He

xx Love, Virtues and Commandments: An Interfaith Perspective

is a savior if we follow his teachings.

5. Prophet Muhammad: called the seal of prophethood by God. His message has testified to the divine message given to previous messengers. He is called "mercy for the worlds," a symbol of love, mercy and grace of God for creation.

The youngest messenger on the scale of time in descending order nurtured, trained and enlightened his faithful companions and honorable members of his family to become models of submission to the divine will. I acknowledge with deepest regards and utmost respect the sublime guidance and exemplary deeds of Prophet Muhammad and his noble companions, guiding us as models, as saints as martyrs serving as the lighthouse for humanity. With great admiration I humbly salute the martyrs who witnessed the supreme sovereignty of the One God by sacrificing their lives on the path of righteousness.

The philosophers, scholars and symbols of morality and nobility in the 20th century who have brightened my heart and soul and saved them from rust and stagnation are: Justice Syed Ameer Ali, a renowned scholar in Islamic history; Alama Sir Muhammad Iqbal, a philosopher-poet of India and Pakistan; Abdullah Yusuf Ali, a scholar in translation of the Holy Quran; Maulana Abu-ul-Kalam Azad, minister of education and a religious leader in India; Allama Syed Ali Naqi, a religious preacher in India; Maulana Abul-Ala Maududi, religious scholar in India and Pakistan; Dr. Seyyed Hossein Nasr, a scholar in Islamic spirituality; Prof. S. Radhakhrisnan, Roa, ex-President of India; Abraham Joshua Herschel, a biblical scholar and philosopher; Maharaj Jagat Singh, my teacher; and Rev. Billy Graham and Rev. Bill Moyers.

The humble efforts on my part, within the limits of human weaknesses, trying to walk on the straight path are indebted to two persons in my life.

1. The guide-posts in my life were the saintly attitudes towards human beings by my late father, Syed Haider. His enormous love and affections for human beings, irrespective of their color, social status, caste or creed, were the architectural designs for me to build a structure for life. He would hold my hand and walk in the lanes of his native village, Massania in northern India. I have vivid memories of how children, men and women, old and young, from various factions, with mild animosities for each other, would come out and embrace him showing love, reverence and appreciation for his love, respect and compassion for all.

2. The dormant seeds broadcasted in my mind and soul by my father were nourished and instilled with new life by Pir Rashid Daula,

a truly, learned and curative physician of ailments of human souls. He broadened my horizons by introducing me to true meanings of divine revelations, unity and universality of One religion of One Creator , and commonality in various faiths.

The acknowledgment of gratitude will not be complete unless I mention a few names of my good friends who encouraged me. I express many thanks to Mr. Thad Kranz, Dr. Muhammad Azarian, Dr. David Roffers, Dr. Harriet Burns, Dr. Dennis Wiechman, Dr. Afak Haydar, Dr. Riaz Zobairi, who are well respected professors in academia and Rabbi Arthur Abrams, a supporter of interfaith, for imparting courage and confidence in me and supporting this effort.

With utmost sincerity I express my gratitude to Dr. Laleh Bakhtiar, a renowned scholar and author in Islamic philosophy , mysticism and educational psychology. She deserves millions of my thanks with commendation for her guidance and support in this endeavor . She edited this manuscript with scholarly perception.

I am deeply indebted to Professor Khalida Rahman and Mrs. Maliha Haider for designing the title, art work and providing pho - tographs in this book. Their highly acclaimed talent has beautified the artistic horizon of the book.

The dearest members of the Haider family, Syed Iftikhar Haider, Dr. Syed Gulzar Haider and Khalida Rahman have deepened my vision and guided me at every phase of this endeavor . They deserve my sincere gratitude. Other members of the family to whom I am indebted are Sughra Haider, Dr. Sajida Haider, Samina Ali, Mubina Ali, Qasim A. Haider, Dr. Syed Abrar Ali, Dr. Kashif Bilal Haider, Dr. Masoom A. Haider, Dr. Mansoor A. Haider, Syed Asad Ali, and Syed Sajid Ali who are worthy of inclusion in this acknowledgment. Their sincere efforts in keeping up my spirits earned deserving recognition from me. I warmly thank Tehmina A. Haider, Fozia Ali , Sarah Ali and Nadia Ali for their enthusiasm and lively interest in this subject while formulating and typing this manuscript. They are my granddaughters who provided incentive and deserve my warmest love, appreciation and best wishes in every aspect of their lives.

PART I
KNOWLEDGE

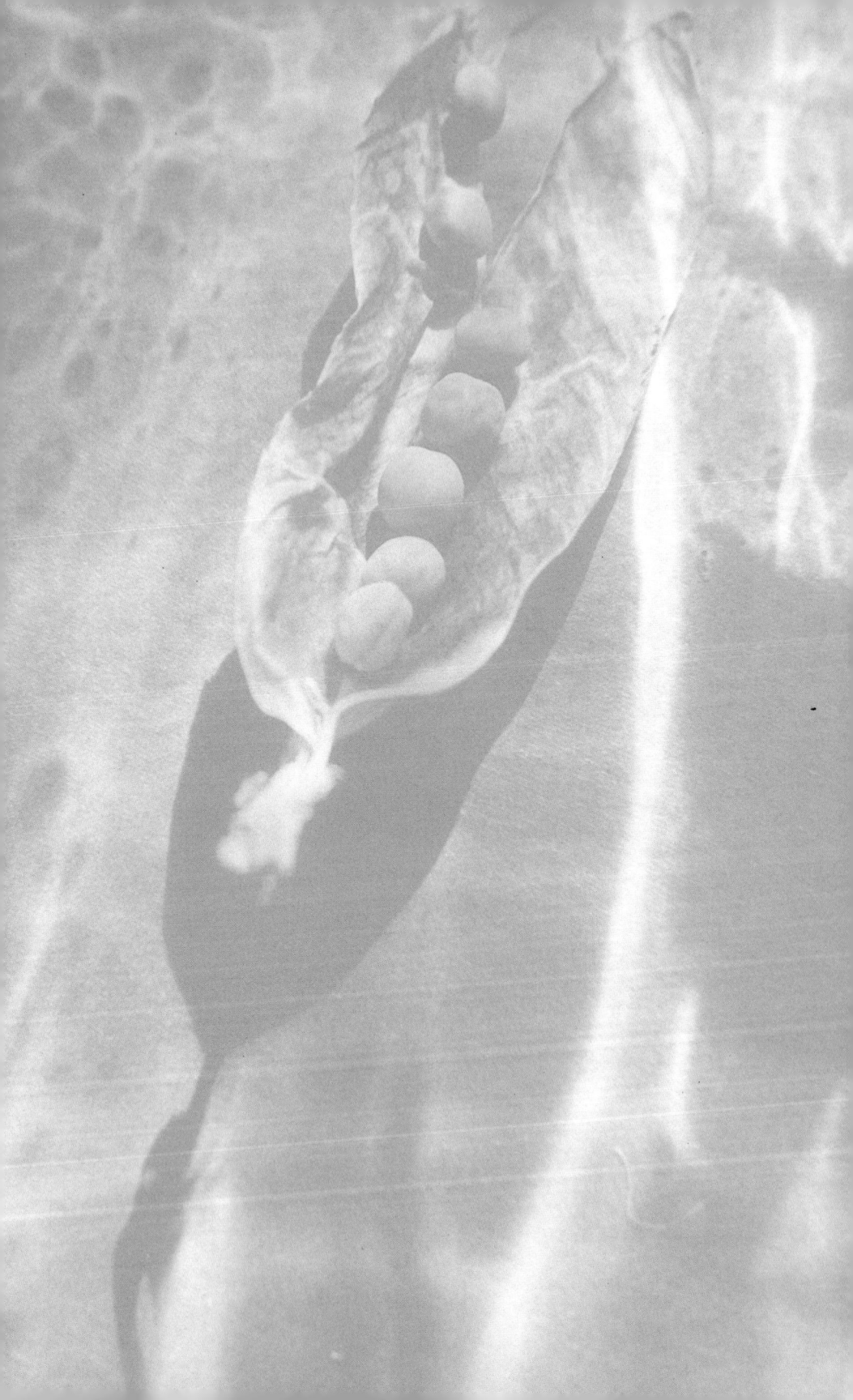

CHAPTER 1
ALMIGHTY GOD

*But You, O Lord, are a God full
of compassion and gracious,
Slow to anger, and plenteous in
mercy and truth.*
—Psalms 86:15—

*Great and marvelous
are Your works, Lord God Almighty!
Just and true are Your ways.*
—Rev 15:36—

*But God, Who is rich in mercy,
because of His Great love with which
He loved us.*
—Eph 2:4—

*And your God
Is One God:*

There is no God but He,
Most Gracious, Most Merciful.
[Quran 2:163]

God is gentle and loves gentleness.
—Prophet Muhammad—

CHAPTER 1
ALMIGHTY GOD

It is in the created nature of the human being, in its pure and unadulterated condition, to feel the existence of his Creator deep in the layers of his soul. But endowed with the faculty of knowing, he seeks to know his God: "Who is my Creator? What is He? Where is He? How can I know Him? Who is He like?"

The human being seeks answers to such questions through his mental faculties. But every effort of the mind keeps reaching its limits at the very boundaries of his intellectual domain. All analogies he can find to describe his God end up being phenomena that in themselves are dependent, perishable, or effects of other causes. In a state of abject helplessness and a touch of despondency at his own limitations, he turns towards the very God he seeks, supplicating, "O Lord, O the One Whom my soul feels but my reason cannot fathom, introduce Your being to me, enlighten my mind so that I may find peace."

Thus through His revelation, descending upon the very heart of His chosen messengers and through the voice of these blessed messengers, God speaks to the human being in words that are understandable, precise, and pure from confusing ambiguities: God is One. He is above every need and desire. His attributes are visible throughout the universe His most admirable, miraculous and fascinating sign is diversity in the nature of creatures, yet with unity of design and harmony in purpose. There is beauty floating on the wings of the rainbow everywhere. The utility of each creature leads us to believe that the highest form of intelligence of the Creator is manifested in the design and purpose of creation. His ability to create is not dependent on any outside factors or on any conditions, or on any special circumstances, or waiting for any means or any special devices. Creation exists as a consequence of His will. His most intelligent and benevolent plans are neither haphazard nor without purpose. God is so illustrious in His power that with perfection He can implement His will with purpose. His design and mission is love, mercy, generosity, benefits and welfare for all His creatures. Anytime He decides upon a thing, His will becomes His command and the thing embraces obedience by coming into existence with an assigned purpose.

> *Verily, when He intends a thing, His Command is, 'Be,' and it is!* [36:82].

The signs of His might, wisdom and gracious altruism are shown through all creation and in all revelations. He has supreme authority over the whole universe. Their very existence of the universe proclaims His power of purposeful creation, His intelligent plan, His combined justice and mercy. The whole universe submits to His will which is manifested in performances of the assigned duties and praises of Almighty God. His glory, power and grace are written on the face of all His creation. The beauty and order of the universe sing His praises. God's wisdom and cognizance are supreme and all-reaching. His knowledge comprehends everything without any veils of time or any demarcation of space. He is independent of space and time but no space and time are without Him. The whole universe is in His presence and under His sovereign rule.

No words are sufficient to describe Him. Human intellectual level cannot do justice in comprehending the Creator's attributes. We can simply say, "There is nothing else like Him. He is the Truth, the Absolute Truth. His grace and His mercy are unbounded." We have no real and true understanding, perception and judgment of His will and plan. One true living God is self-subsisting, perfect, eternal from the beginning and eternal to the end, with infinite existence and unequivocal reality. His attributes cannot and must not be assigned to any fabrication of our illusory minds.

He is the Creator Who shaped the heavens and earth without any precedent. He is the Form-giver, Who is independent of any need to copy preexistent models. No mind can construct an analogy for Him nor is there any vision that can fully see the glory of His boundless majesty. There is nothing in all existence that is like Him. All metaphors remain feeble human attempts in describing Him. It is in this sense that no human relationship nor emotion can be ascribed to Him. He is not parented by anyone nor is He anyone's parent. It is beyond His glory to have a wife and human-like plans for a family, nor is He subject to desirous, jealous, temperamental and capricious lapses. His being is free of partnerships. He is solitary, unique, indivisible, and eternally One.

He is generous in composing His signs and marvels across the canvas of His Creation. The firmament is studded with twinkling stars. A contemplative moon gently swims across the night. Clouds of various shapes are carried by the invisible winds. The colors of dawn herald yet another day's solar sojourn. The shadows elongate, shrink and elongate again and another display of dusk colors sends off the solar chariots beyond the horizon. The winds carry on their shoulders the clouds of various shapes, sometimes gently, other times with splitting ferocity, and only with His divine permission, they let go of their water. Thus the thirsty and the despondent earth joyously puts forth green life, affirming in silent eloquence the mercy, the glory and the power of God. All the constituents of nature are positioned in their rightful places. All are embarked on their destined courses, in complete obedience. The cosmic clockwork of nature, and this law-abiding carousel of creation, demonstrates this heavenly display of God's mercy that enlightens the seeker's path and strengthens the faith of the pious.

God has insisted upon human knowledge to study, rationalize and meditate about His creation and purpose behind it by using deep intellectual perception. Every increase of light on the horizon of scientific studies reveals the handiwork of the most intelligent Creator. God's mastery in creation is manifested in every phase of nature. Human faculties to observe, think and meditate are invited for realization of the realism in existence of One unique God.

With the dawn of scientific age, breathtaking discoveries have been made in spite of scientific limitations. The abilities in the human mind for logical inductions and deductions, seeing, knowing, realizing and rationalizing, establishing relationships between cause and effect and orderly arranging the links of thought processes have laid the sound foundations in awareness of God. This knowledge, impregnated with faith in Him, has turned the human soul into a blooming and flourishing garden. It has escorted the humanity discovering the ways out of darkness into the light of divine guidance Who bestowed the human mind with sparks of universal intelligence: The divine message? Human reasoning and scientific endeavors are gifts from the Creator imparting superiority over other creatures. Human beings can observe thoughtfully, probe and edit various inflows of knowledge. They realize the existence of God. The sparks of universal intelligence are asking: "Behold! all around you are marvelously scattered the signs of His useful and purposeful creation."

The Creator of an orderly, harmonious and systematic universe deserves all the praise. The origin, structure, size and age of this orderly universe, submissive to laws of nature, are amazingly beyond human comprehension. It transcends ordinary means of measurements. The time-space relationship in the boundless universe is a challenge to human intelligence, asking us to bow to God, the Creator of the Universe, with all humbleness, realizing and accepting His Being. With restricted knowledge and limited boundaries of the human mind it has been revealed that the universe is magnificent, sumptuous and super abounding, but still restricted by laws and decrees. The adorned facts create fanciful and reverential wonders in the human mind. The dimensions of the orderly universe are so enormously large that measurement by units of distance, meters or miles, is futile and impossible. It is measured with the speed of light (in one second a beam of light travels 186,000 miles).

How many galaxies are in the universe? How many stars are in each galaxy? The only spiritual realization that emerges from this awesome complexity, vastness of this impenetrable diversity and orderly functioning with fine distinctions is that there was, is, and always will be a divine hand of Creator, designing, making, actualizing, rearing, fashioning, providing, nourishing and nurturing this vast universe with assigned purpose and schema.

Life is a miracle, an endowment, and an inspiration from God. It is an integral part of obedience which came into existence on a command from God. Tremendous essentials and scrupulous conditions are requisite for the throbbing and survival of life on this planet. All these factors, their interdependence and multitudes of their proper relationships are not possible by chance. Life does not start as an accident. Nothing comes into being by itself. God creates everything. He is the active force behind the whole creation. He gives life, maintains it, and supports it. He ordains laws to regulate and govern the creation. Everything follows an appointed course and is busy in fulfilling the purpose of creation. The properties assigned to various elements establish a link between cause and effect. Yet the complexity of even a single organism cannot be explained. Millions of different species have appeared on this earth. Each living organism is bestowed with some degree of wisdom, the ability to survive the hostilities in the environment and to perform the assigned duties. Special arrangements are made by the Creator to compensate some shortcomings.

One of the most amazing facts of creation is an evidence that all lives are related to each other. Our common ancestor is the first single cell. Who has granted the miraculous properties to protoplasm and ultra-microscopic genes that completely rule all life on earth? The capabilities of life to accomplish its purpose of creation is a unmistakable proof of the most altruistic Creator with all-pervading intelligence. He provides sustenance to every from of life. He creates life and supports every phase of it. His generosity is inexhaustible and encompasses every creature.

The interdependence of organism in a rain forest is a mystery in the study of ecosystems. The sparkling light and buzzing sound of life in every form fascinates the human mind. For all practical purposes there is no wind within the rain forest. In this atmosphere wind pollination is not possible. Nature strategizes the pollination in a superior way by using moving creatures.

Each organism created by the most benevolent Creator is equipped with survival skills. Insects that are capable of outlasting winter in cold regions do so in a hardened resting stage. Some accumulate fat in the body fluid so that ice crystals cannot be formed. The best natural antifreeze used by some insects is glycerol. The grass family in the prairies has wind-pollinated flowers. In the rain forest grasses develop bright flowers to attract insects. Sometimes even bright colors do not suffice. Nature provides additional strong attractive scents to flowers luring the insects. Who makes such arrangements for continuous pulsating of life in various forms? Many desert plants make special arrangements to conserve limited amount of water during hot dry summers. They acquire carbon dioxide during night to present it for photosynthesis the following day. This arrangement keeps their pores closed during the heat of the day. Who provides this mechanism in the plants to survive hostility of weather? A hibernating ground squirrel adjusts the internal biological clock to drop the body temperature close to freezing. The heartbeat slows down tremendously. Who teaches them the adjustment in the internal biological clocks? How do such clocks keep time in the physiology of well-planned ecological engineering?

Who instills in the minds of newly hatched turtles to leave the sand nests and run toward sea where life will embrace and swim with them. How do they receive inspiration with warnings that death will be waiting for them if they run toward the desert. Who draws in minute details a navigation map on the tiny brains of migratory birds. They cover thousands of miles

flying over land and sea to reach their destination after fulfilling the assigned duties. Who directs and oversees salmon leaving the darkness of the sea water and coming back to its own
river, traveling up the very side of the river into which flows the
tributary where he was born? What brings him back with flaw-
less precision? Where does this guiding propulsion originate?
Who navigates him? Who has sculptured in different forms and
shapes all living things? Who has designed every leaf of every
tree? Who has painted different designs of colors on flowers?
Who has taught birds to sing in praise of their Creator and com-
municate with each other in enchanting music of varying musi-
cal notes? The truth that humans have been honored with abilities to conceive the idea of Almighty God is in itself a unparalleled proof of His benevolence.

Human life, the so called pride of creation due to the intri-
cate marvels of the human brain, starts with a single cell (ovum
fertilized by a sperm). The same four nucleotides spell out the
hereditary design with instructions for making a particular
organism. In spite of this commonality in the language of four
worded genetic code, every life form on this globe comes into
existence with a different set of genetic instructions. In fact it is
the sequence of the four nucleotides along either of the con-
stituent strands of DNA that is responsible for the variety in
life. Human DNA is a ladder, twisted into a helix, laden with a
billion (an estimated figure) nucleotides. The chances of arranging these nucleotides in varying sequence and order are astro-
nomically immense. That is why two human beings are never
alike. Their finger prints and the patterns on their irises (rain-
bows) in the eyes are never identical. We have to believe that
every organism is meticulously created by a great designer,
Who has a different pattern for each living organism. The
guardian-Lord brings us into being. He bestows on us faculties,
fraternities and forms required to fulfill the expected purpose of
our creation. He creates in our environments all the essentials
for sustenance of our lives, providing with needed order and
preparation.

Human life carries a special status because it bears a crown of vice royalty. Human beings are equipped gratuitously with the ability to exercise limited free-will. He has instituted the divine laws and decrees and conveyed them to human beings through His appointed messengers. The divine guidance can lead us to salvation. He has endowed us with intuitions, physical and psychological inclinations which are suitable to meet the demands of His laws and decrees. He guides us perpetually through the institution of prophethood so that we are not at the total mercy of mechanical laws. Thus we should be using God-given intelligence to differentiate between right and wrong. We should be able to exercise our limited will in the light of divine-guidance and thus receive His grace, mercy and love by achieving high status destined for human beings. The prospects which divine guidance opens up for human beings are spreading and extending up to the boundaries of heaven. The most astonishing and pleasureful fact is that God is everywhere and in everything but no where so close as in human hearts. All the wonderful complex, circuitous and cryptic forms of creation with different gradations and awesome subtlety that we find in creation are mingled under one universal umbrella that obeys laws of the Creator and follows a well established order for the systematic disposition of their assigned roles.

In the light of the verses from the Holy Quran, A. Yusuf Ali describes:

> But the Signs of God are everywhere in creation. The sun and the shadow, the day and the night, the wind and the rain—all things in nature are symbols, and point to the law divine, and the destiny, good or ill, of man. Will he not learn and put his trust in Him, the Merciful? His true servants ever adore him in humility and fear of wrong, in faith and just moderation in life, in respect for duties owed to God and men and self, in avoidance of all that is false or futile, in strict and grateful attention to God's Message, and in the wish to put themselves and their families in the van of those who love and honor God.[1]

The whole creation has a purpose, merit and serviceability.

It fits into a design. It carries truth in every sense of the word. It manifests goodness based on His justice. The design has no freakness or mere fun of sport. We see, appreciate and admire the glory of the heavens and the earth. The stretches of human imagination creates wondrous excitement. We bow our heads before the Creator in astonishment. He is not a capricious deity in a playful sport with creation. All His creation, and there is nothing that escapes being His creation, brings with it its inherently imbued purpose. All parts of creation are harmoniously linked within a grand, interdependent, comprehensive, disciplined and purposeful schema. He is the ultimate source of all conceptions of value, of goodness, of beauty. The human intellect can know Him only through His divine attributes. There is no separation between Him and His attributes which He has chosen for Himself and revealed to us through His chosen messengers. Thus all praise, be it for Him or for any aspect of any member of His creation, is ultimately referred to Him.

Syed Ameer Ali in his book, *The Spirit of Islam,* summarizes, the attributes of Almighty God:

> God is: All-mighty, the All-knowing, the All-just, the Lord of the worlds, the Author of the heavens and the earth, the Creator of life and death, in whose hand is dominion and irresistible power; the great, all-powerful Lord of the glorious Throne. God is the Mighty, the Strong, the Most High, the Producer, the Maker, the Fashioner, the Wise, the Just, the True, the Swift in reckoning, who knows every ant's weight of good and of ill that each man hath done, and who suffers not the reward of the faithful to perish. But the Almighty, the All-wise, is also the King, the Holy, the Peaceful, the Faithful, the Guardian over His servants, the Sheltered of the orphan, the Guide of the erring, the Deliverer from every affliction, the Friend of the bereaved, the Consoler of the afflicted; in His hand is good, and He is the generous Lord, the Gracious, the Hearer, the Near-at-Hand, the Compassionate, the Merciful, the Very-forgiving, whose love for man is more tender than that of the mother-bird for her young.[2]

Almighty God is our creator and cherisher. We have deficiencies, defects and defilements. In spite of these shortcomings we have faith in His forgiveness. He forgives us if we beg, not on our merits but purely on His grace. He is the listener of the repentant soul, the forgiver of the returning prodigal, the merciful Lord of all. He is the giver of a new life and bestower of hope on all those who, having gone to the limits of hedonistic self-worship, self-indulgence, and exploitation of the fellow human, turn helplessly and sincerely towards Him. The warm and healing mantle of His forgiving mercy envelopes the wounded souls and suffering bodies of those who return towards Him.

In light of the verses from The Holy Quran, A. Yusuf Ali has described:

> Words of God: His wonderful Signs and Commandments are infinite and cannot be expressed if all the trees were made into pens, and all the wide Ocean, multiplied seven times were made into ink. Any Book of His revelation would deal with matters which man can understand and use in his life: there are mysteries beyond mysteries that man can never fathom. Nor would any praise that we could write with infinite resources be adequate to describe His power, glory and wisdom."[3]

The divine attributes of God permeate the body of Old Testament, New Testament and the Quranic text as profusely and pervasively as light permeate space. The cognizance of God illuminates the mind as the reader, slowly and thoughtfully, recites and contemplates on the verses of these revelations. An effort has been made to quote a few verses in the attached table as indication of a commonality in His attributes in the scriptures. A few quotations from the Traditions of Prophet Muhammad, sayings of Hazrat Ali, and other books of wisdom are included in this chapter after the table.

VERSES ON ALMIGHTY GOD

THE OLD TESTAMENT

Hear, O Israel: The Lord our God, the Lord is One.
Duet. 6:4

I am the First and I am the Last and beside Me there is no God.
Isa 44:6

How great are His signs! And how mighty are His wonders! His kingdom is an everlasting kingdom and His dominion is from generation to generation.
Dan 3:33

Yours, O Lord, is the greatness, the power, the glory, the victory, the majesty; for all that is in the heavens and in the earth is Yours. Yours is the kingdom, O Lord and You are exalted as head above all.
I Chr 29:11

Did you not know? Have you not heard that the everlasting God, the Lord, the Creator of the ends of the earth, faints not neither is weary? His discernment is past searching out.
Isa 40:28

You are the Lord, even You alone. You have made heaven, the heaven of heavens, with all their host, the earth and all things that are thereon, the seas and all that is in them and You preserved them all and the host of heaven worships You.
Neh 9:6

THE NEW TESTAMENT

Jesus answered him, "The first of all the commandments is: 'Hear, O Israel, the Lord our God, the Lord is one.'"
Mark 12:29

Now to the King eternal, immortal, invisible, to God Who alone is wise, with honor and glory forever and ever. Amen.
1 Tim 1:17

For of Him and through Him and to Him are all things, to whom be glory forever and ever. Amen.
Rom 11:36

God, Who made the world and everything in it since He is Lord of heaven and earth, does not dwell in temples made with hands. Nor is He worshiped with men's hands as though He needed anything since He gives to all life, breath and all things.
Acts 17:24, 25

And I heard, as it were, the voice of a great magnitude, as the sound of many waters and as the sound of mighty thunderings saying, "Alleluia! For the Lord God Omnipotent reigns!"
Rev 19:6

And there is no creature hidden from His sight, but all things are naked and open to the eyes of Him to whom we must give account.
Heb 4:13

THE QURAN

God is He, with Whom there is no other god; Who knows all things both secret and open; He Most Gracious, Most Merciful.
59:22

God is He with Whom there is no other god; the Sovereign, the Holy One, the Source of Peace [and Perfection], the Guardian of Faith, the Preserver of Safety, the Exalted in Might, the Irresistible, the Supreme; Glory be to God above the partners they attribute to Him.
59:23

He is God, the Creator, the Evolver, the Bestower of Forms, to Him belong the Most Beautiful Names. Whatever is in the heavens and on earth declares His praises and glory. He is the Exalted in Might, the Wise.
59:24.

And if all the trees on earth were pens and the ocean [were ink], with seven oceans behind to add to its [supply], yet would not the words of God be exhausted for God is Exalted in power, full of wisdom.
31:26-27

God is the Light of the heavens and the earth.
29:35

Verses on Almighty God

The Old Testament

You are great, O Lord God, for there is none like You, neither is there any God beside You.

II Sam 7:22

But You, O Lord, are a God full of compassion and gracious, slow to anger and plenteous in mercy and truth.

PSA 86:15

The Lord is righteous in all His ways and gracious in all His works.

PSA 145:17

Who made heaven and earth, the sea and all that is in them; Who keeps truth forever; Who executes justice for the oppressed; Who gives bread to the hungry. The Lord loosens the prisoners; the Lord opens the eyes of the blind; the Lord raises up them that are bowed down; the Lord loves the righteous.

PSA 147:5

Who covers the heaven with clouds, Who prepares rain for the earth, Who makes the mountains to spring with grass.

PSA 147:8

The New Testament

Nevertheless He did not leave Himself without witness, in that He did good, gave us rain from heaven and fruitful seasons, filling our hearts with food and gladness.

Acts 14:17

He makes His sun rise on the evil and on the good, and sends rain on the just and on the unjust.

Matt 5:45

I am the Alpha and the Omega, the Beginning and the End, the First and the Last.

Rev 22:13

Great and marvelous are Your works, Lord God Almighty! Just and true are Your ways, O King of the saints! Who shall not fear You, O Lord, and glorify Your name? For You alone are holy. For all nations shall come and worship before You, for Your judgments have been manifested.

Rev 15:34

Who alone has immortality, dwelling in unapproachable light, whom no man has seen or can see, to whom be honor and everlasting power. Amen.

I Tim 1:17

The Quran

He is the First and the Last and the Manifest and the Hidden and He has knowledge of all things.

57:3

God! There is no god but He, the Living, the Self-subsisting, Eternal. No slumber can seize Him nor sleep. His are all things in the heavens and on earth.

2:255

For God is He Who gives all Sustenance. Lord of Power, steadfast forever.

51:58

Then Praise be to God, Lord of the heavens and Lord of the earth, Lord and Cherisher of all the worlds! To Him be glory throughout the heavens and the earth and He is exalted in Power, full of Wisdom!

45:36-37

SAYINGS ON ALMIGHTY GOD

Adore God as you would if you saw Him; for , if you see Him not, He sees you.

Verily God is more compassionate towards His creatures than a mother towards her own child.

If you put your whole trust in God, as you ought, He most certainly will give you sustenance, as He gives to the birds when they come out hungry in the morning, but return full to their nests.

Worship God and associate none with him.

There is no god but God.

Traditions of Prophet Muhammad

All praise and glory is due to the Lord, Whose W orth cannot be described even by the greatest rhetoricians of all times; Whose Blessings and Bounties cannot be enumerated by reck - oners and enumerators of all ages, and homage due to Him can - not be adequately paid even by the most assiduous and perse - vering attempters. None can fully understand or explain His Being however hard he may try. Reason and sagacity cannot visualize Him. Intelligence, understanding and attainment can - not attain the depth of knowledge to study or scrutinize the supreme sovereign. Human faculties of conception, perception and learning, and attributes of volition, intuition and appre - hension cannot catch sight of His person or fathom the extent of His might and glory. His attributes cannot be fixed, limited or defined. There do not exist words in any language to specify or define His qualities, peculiarities, characteristics and singular - ities. As His being is eternal, therefore, no time could be imag - ined to say that He existed since then, similarly no period could be assigned for duration of His existence. Who accepts His attributes to be separate from Him, he forsakes the idea of unity of God and believes in duality. Such a person in fact believes Him to exist in parts.

Ali ibn Abu Talib

Brahman, the Supreme Reality, the Absolute, which transcends time, space, and causality and cannot be comprehended by human thought or rendered in words. His form is not an object of vision; no one beholds Him with the eye. His glory prevails on earth, in heaven, in His own seat, the holy city of the heart. He looks at all things; knows all things. All things, their nourishment, their names, their forms, are from His will. All that He has willed is right.

The Upanishads

There is but One God, Eternal Truth, Almighty Creator, Unfearful, Without Hate and Enmity, Immortal Entity, Unborn, Self-Existent, By His Grace, shalt thou worship the One Who was True before the creation, the One Who was True in the beginning of the creation, the One Who is True now, and O Nanak, The One Who shall be True for ever.

He cannot be installed like an idol nor can man shape His likeness.

Guru Nanak

CHAPTER 2
CHARACTERISTICS OF THE
UNIVERSAL TRUTH

*You shall diligently keep the commandments
of the Lord your God and His testimonies
and His statutes which He
has commanded you.*
—Deut 6:17—

We ought to obey God rather than men.
—Acts 5:29—

*If you keep My commandments
You shall abide in love.*
—John 15:10—

*We sent not a prophet except
[to teach] in the language of his
[own] people in order to make*

[things] clear to them.
—[Quran 14:4]—

Not a prophet did We send before you
[O Muhammad] without this inspiration
sent by Us to him: that there is no god
but I. Therefore worship and serve Me.
—[Quran 21:25]—

I would not have the whole wealth of the world
in the place of this revelation.
—Prophet Muhammad—

CHAPTER 2
CHARACTERISTICS OF THE
UNIVERSAL TRUTH

Memory and superior intelligence are the gifts of the Creator which distinguish human beings from other creatures. With this memory and thinking comes the opposing tendency of forgetfulness and stupidity. The entire drama of human existence can be imagined in what he remembers to employ for its utility. Whatever he considers worthy of remembering and how he constructs rituals to remember it identifies its value, and whatever he allows himself to forget indicates his rejection of that.

God's signs are all over and everywhere in the universe. He bestowed human beings with a living conscience and has sent His messengers to the whole human race since the human appearance on this planet. The messengers brought the divine message in the language of their people. The essence of the message is to obey His laws. The messengers call their people in a clear, understandable language of the people to do good and to stay away from evil. The human race cannot present any excuse that God has abandoned them or He does not care about their salvation. His divine grace and mercy invite them to choose the right path by following His laws. The universality in divine Truth is manifested in unity of the divine message assigned to all of His messengers sent to all the nations during varying times in the history of mankind. His justice is evident. The source of the message in One. The messengers are chosen by One God. Human needs are the same. The means and sources of salvation are the same. The right has never been wrong and the evil can never embrace the right. Therefore, how can there be a difference in the divine message.

All true messengers of God preached the true gospel of unity.

Ameer Ali has quoted the Quran to prove the universality of God's message:

> Verily those who believe (Muslims) and those who are Jews, Christians, or Sabaeans, whoever has faith in God and the last day (future existence) and works that which is right and good, for them shall be the reward with their Lord; there will come no fear on them; neither shall they be grieved.[1]

The criteria for judging the wholeness of an all-embracing religion are practicability, enduring influence on the common relations of mankind in a healthy structure of social life, and a positive influence on everyday life in the light of rationalistic practicability.

Ameer Ali mentioned the universality of God's religion,

> A religion of right-doing, right-thinking, and right-speaking, founded on divine love, universal charity, and the man in the sight of the Lord.[2]

> Excepting for the conception of the sonship of Jesus, there is no fundamental difference between Christianity and Islam. In their essence they are one and the same; both are the outcome of the same spiritual forces working in humanity.[3]

The spiritual awakening with beams of light illuminating the soul elevates the human being from the levels of sensual animality to higher stages of humanity. He becomes free from the syndicated hold of materialistic values.

This faith in spiritual guidance is the most dominant power ruling human beings' intellectual abilities and guiding them in the direction of truth and morality. The love of God is love of spiritual values: It is the love of the religion. It is love for other human beings and other creatures: It is the way of life prescribed by God for human beings through His divine messages. It should subjugate all other love for worldly benefits and selfish aspirations influenced by greed and niggardness. It is not a sentimental style. It is bounded on the everlasting relationship between a Creator and His humble, obedient, and subservient creation. It is a covenant with God to obey His commands forever. This covenant is based on love of the most merciful God. It raises human beings above selfish desires and passions. All the actions are motivated and engineered by one consideration, the desire to gain His pleasure and His grace by obeying Him and only Him. Even the precious life which is His gift is sacrificed in His way in performance of prescribed duties to enlist oneself in the ranks of His most obedient servants. Thus, all activities under this love become acts of worship. This divine message designs and shapes the human beings who formulates a society through this message which is deeply incorporated in every aspect of human life.

This religion of humanity rejects all forms, types, and shades of prejudice, discrimination, and distinctions based on socio-economic classes, nationality, color, creed, and man-made differences in religions.

Human beings are created under the same laws of creation, therefore, the true religion of God Who has created every human being under the same laws is for the benefit of human kind. God's patterns do not change nor does the truth that originates from Him. All His messengers and deputed guides, who hold the messengership, the station of being the medium, and true exemplifiers of guidance from the God, have two essential dimensions. The first dimension is that of the "bringer of glad tidings" of the beneficence and mercy of God, the hope, the light, the law, the criteria between truth and falsehood and finally the bounteous rewards that await the followers of the guidance, the obedient ones to His commandments and the subservient ones to the will of the Lord. The second dimension is that of the messengers being the "warners" against the deceptions that originate from within and without the human mind. Under the satanic influences, the tendencies to follow the desires of power, pleasure and wealth promote defiance of all commandments. The grievous punishments await the deniers of Truth, the rebellious and the arrogant ones, and the worshippers of false deities.

"Warners" and "bringers of glad-tidings" reinforce and confirm one another. It would be a folly, and a contradiction to the very concept of the eternal and All-Wise God to even imagine that He would send two different guidances and two mutually belligerent guides. The revealed Books ask human beings to use intelligence in believing the Truth which is reinforced and confirmed by the signs to be seen in visible nature. Yusuf Ali explained a few verses from the Quran:

> Revelation leads mankind from the depths of darkness into light. It comes to every age and nation in its own language. So was it before; so is it always. The apostles were doubted, insulted, threatened, and persecuted, but their trust was sure in God. It is evil that will be wiped out. God's Truth is as a goodly tree, firmly established on its roots, stretching its branches high and wide, and bearing good fruit at all times.[4]

One of the characteristics of the divine message is that it is free and all inclusive for the human race. God's grace is entirely under His command and control. He shows it in accordance with His most wise scheme and will. No human mind can assign any limits and boundaries to His grace. There is only one true religion, the message of the One God. It is embodied in total submission to the will of God, which is translated into His laws and decrees.

God has sent His messengers with this one divine message to all nations in the language of their people. His benign justice is characterized by the oneness of the message toward humanity in all ages since humans were created on this earth. The same message was preached by Prophets Noah, Abraham, Moses, Jesus and Muhammad (salutations and peace be upon all His messengers). There is no difference in the religions and the preachings of all the prophets. Some are mentioned in the Old Testament, some in the New Testament, and some in the Quran. Other names are not mentioned but belief in prophethood is commanded by One God.

The dogma of mysticism is that "there is one temple in the universe and that is the body of man."[4] A.Yusuf Ali mentions the gift of God in the light of verses from the Quran:

> Among the highest and greatest of the gifts of God is His Revelation, which is the Criterion by which we may judge between right and wrong—between false and true worship, between the Message that comes from God and the forgeries of men, between the Real in our eternal future and the fancies by which we are misled. The messengers of God come as men to live among men and guide them.[5]

The illuminated minds and the souls of His messengers direct human beings to a higher form of existence. When the curtains fall, the eternal life embraces the believers instead of the doom of death. They receive tidings for a home in heaven. This is the reward for listening, accepting and obeying in deeds His divine message. In practice they turn their mind, soul and deeds away from the bondage of corruption and thus achieve final victory over death and sin.

There is a logic behind this faith in the truism of prophethood and in unity of the divine message throughout the history of human beings. All the prophets, some names have been mentioned, some names are not known in the written account of human history, preached the same divine message. The name of the divine message carries the same meaning in every language of the message. The submission to His will, His laws, and His commands is incorporated in the divine message. This submission is the foundation of true peace in the human soul, between his Creator and the created and is called 'Islam' in Arabic. God's religion in languages of other nations must have a name in that language describing the meaning as peace by submission to His will.

In the Quran the One God has used the Arabic word 'Islam' for His eternal and universal religion of submission to His will, His laws, and His commandments. He has mentioned the names of some prophets clearly stating that the religion of God brought by Prophets Noah, Abraham, Ishmael, Isaac, Jacob, Moses, David, Solomon, Jesus and Muhammad, peace be upon them all, was *islam* in the Arabic language,that the followers by total submission to His laws and decrees were called *muslims* in the Arabic language and that there was no difference in the religion preached by God-sent-messengers. It is a question of common sense and a challenge to human intelligence to ponder deeply about this divine message and find the unity, commonality, and universality in the message.

There is one great command to submit to His will, the only Truth. However, human beings created different labels of the religions professed by them because under the pretext of these various labels they can find so many excuses to hate other human beings causing wars, bloodshed, and destruction. God's message is not for the creation of any sect or for the claims of superiority by any ethnic religion or for the benefit and superiority of a particular race. If His sun shines for everybody, if His rain brings life to the parched soil and thirsty crops, if He does not discriminate between who believes in Him and who does not, while showering sweet water upon all, if He creates every human being under the same biological laws with the same physical and spiritual needs, if He provides all those needs, and if He has created all the essentials for the sustenance of life in every form on this earth, free of charge, then it is the most unscrupulous thought, totally lacking in conscience, that the Most Merciful and the Most Compassionate has not provided guidance for the salvation of every human soul. The logic demands to believe that all divine revelations at different intervals on the scale of time in the history of man lead to one religion, for the Truth is one, which was preached by all the prophets. It is a joyful submission to His will. This faith in the mortality of the totally sinful life and immortality of life in obedience to His will is a guiding light to reach the enthroned destination in heaven after sailing through the treacherous waters on this earth.

This short life on earth receives assurance from this faith that death has been deprived of its injurious effects. Life will receive final victory over death. A faithful servant of God, in spite of outward hardships, difficulties and hurdles in every way enjoys the short stay on this earth. He is full of love, beauty, and wisdom. He looks around and finds purpose, harmony and radiant beauty all over. There are images of God's attributes in the beautifully designed, gracefully formulated, worthwhile, and purposeful creation. With exalted mental and moral qualities he perceives this life on earth as a road to heaven.

In spite of human cruelty and injustice, the havoc of wars and horrors of strife, human beings enjoy a fragrance of blooming gardens inside. They can find the glitter of love, purity and sincerity, through eternal values. As Prophet Jesus said, "Blessed are the pure in heart, for they shall see God."

Love is the most pious, pure, and blessed thing in human experience. It is the only source and course to create contacts with the attributes of God. Prophet Jesus said, "He prays best who loves best." It is planted in the seed beds of eternal grace and bloom in pure obedient souls. Its bright flame cannot be extinguished by any of the changes and chances of mortal life. The many facets of submission to His will are peace, love, greetings, safety, and salvation. It is never ending striving after righteousness. The foundation is laid with belief in the oneness of God, in all His attributes, in immateriality of the worldly worth, charity and welfare for other human beings, cultivating brotherhood in mankind, enslaving the passions, expressing gratitude with love and humbleness to the Giver of everything; and accountability of every human thought and deed.

Ameer Ali quotes the Quran, describing the characteristics of human beings who embrace and obey His divine message as His will.

> *The servants of the Merciful are they that walk upon the earth softly; and when the ignorant speak unto them, they reply, "Peace!" they that spend the night worshiping their Lord, prostrate, and standing, and resting: those that, when they spend, are neither profuse nor niggardly, but take a middle course: those that invoke not with God any other God, and slay not a soul that God has forbidden otherwise than by right; and commit not fornication: . . . they who bear not witness to that which is false; and when they pass by vain sport, they pass it by with dignity: who say, "Oh, our Lord, grant us of our wives and children such as shall be a comfort unto us, and make us examples unto the pious,"—these shall be the reward, for that they persevered; and they shall be accosted in paradise with welcome and salutation:—forever therein,—a fair abode and resting place! [25:63-76].*

One of the characteristics of the divine message is that it is sublime, clear, and easy to understand, sent in the everyday language to the people through a messenger who lived with them and served as a model of piety, devotion, holiness, love, compassion, wisdom and purity in mind, soul, and deeds. A splendid harmony exists in the words of that messenger and in his deeds. The unambiguous message in simple and clear words is evident by studying the basic principles of different religions.[6]

Few examples may suffice this mental apprehension about the exactness, unmistakability and openness to the understanding of every human being. Who has problems in comprehending the direct and simple commandments, common threads in every religion, a true foundation of the faith, a clear and simple measure of accountability with perfect reliability and validity. Those commandments which are considered essential for the health and welfare of human society and which have never been changed because of their sublime role in developing and rewarding interpersonal relationships in the society are: "you shall not steal," "you shall not commit murder," "you shall not commit adultery," "you shall have no other gods before Me," "honor your father and your mother," "give to him who asks you," "love your God," "you shall love your neighbor."

What is so complex or hard to understand or hard to follow in these commandments? Is there anybody amongst humans who have not heard these commandments? The details of these commandments with the logic embodied in them and with their consequences are discussed in the next chapters.

Another characteristic of the divine revelation is that there is good news, a gospel for those who listen, accept and obey. In case of pitfalls or shortcomings, human beings repent and beg for mercy. There are tidings of forgiveness and mercy. Also, there are warnings in the revelations for thoughtless, negligent, inconsiderate, rebellious, disobedient, and arrogant human beings.

Yusuf Ali, in the light of verses from the Quran, describes characteristics of the message and the faithful ones who obey:

> The best of people is the person of faith who calls all people to share his faith. Is the will of God. Eschew all evil, and adore God, and Him alone. His signs are everywhere, and His message is the same through all the ages, a guide and a healing to those who believe. Dispute not, but live righteousness. Knowledge belongs to God, but falsehood deprives man of hope, humility, and clear sight, and drives him to hypocrisy. So turn to Truth, and live.[7]
>
> The brotherhood of Truth is one in all ages: It is narrow men who create sects. Let them not think that the goods of this world can shield them from evil or its consequences. God's Truth and His messenger can be known to all: for He in His Mercy has given us faculties and judgment, if we would but use them. The message is not new: all creation proclaims it: High above all is the Lord of glory supreme![8]

VERSES ON CHARACTERISTICS OF UNIVERSAL TRUTH

THE OLD TESTAMENT

O Lord, the God of Abraham, of Isaac, and of Israel, our fathers, keep this forever, even the imagination of the thoughts of the heart of Your people and direct their heart unto You; and give unto Solomon, my son, a whole heart to keep Your commandments, Your testimonies, and Your statutes, and to do all these things and to build the palace for which I have made provision.

I Chr 29:18-19

The Lord is God and has given us light. Order the festival procession with boughs even unto the horns of the altar.

PSA 118:27

O house of Jacob, come and let us walk in the light of the Lord.

Isa 2:5

Arise, shine, for your light is come and the glory of the Lord is risen upon you.

Isa 60:1

THE NEW TESTAMENT

Do not think that I came to destroy the Law or the Prophets. I did not come to destroy but to fulfill.

Matt 5:17

Whom heaven must receive until the times of restoration of all things which God has spoken by the mouth of all His holy prophets since the world began.

Acts 3:21

For Moses truly said to the fathers, 'The Lord your God will raise up for you a prophet like me from your brethren. Him you shall hear in all things, whatever He says to you. And it shall be that every soul who will not hear that prophet shall be utterly destroyed from among the people. Yes, and all the prophets, from Samuel and those who follow, as many as have spoken, have also foretold these days. You are sons of the prophets and of the covenant with God made with our fathers, saying to Abraham, "And in your seed all the families of the earth shall be blessed." To you first, God, having raised up His servant Jesus, sent Him to bless you, in turning away every one of you from your inequities.

Acts 3:22-26

THE QURAN

There has come to you from God a new light and a perspicuous Book wherewith God guides all who seek His good pleasure to ways of peace and safety, and leads them out of darkness, by His Will, unto the light, guides them to a path that is Straight.

5:17-18

Say: 'We believe in God and the revelation given to us and to Abraham, Ismail, Isaac, Jacob, and the tribes and that are given to Moses and Jesus and that are given to all prophets from their Lord: We make no distinction between one and another of them and we bow to God (in *islam*).'

2:136

It was We who revealed the law (to Moses): therein was guidance and light. By its standard have been judged the Jews, by the prophets who bowed (as in *islam*) to God's will, by the rabbis and the religious scholars.

5:47

We gave Moses the Book and followed him up with a succession of Messengers. We gave Jesus, the son of Mary, clear signs and strengthened him with the holy spirit.

2:87

VERSES ON CHARACTERISTICS OF UNIVERSAL TRUTH

THE OLD TESTAMENT

Know, therefore, that the Lord your God, He is God; the faithful God, who keeps covenant and mercy with them that love Him and keeps His commandments to a thousand generations; and repays them that hate Him to their face, to destroy them; He will not be slack to him that hates Him, He will repay him to his face. You shall therefore keep the commandment and the statutes, and the ordinances which I command you this day, to do them.

Deut 7:9, 10, 11

That you might fear the Lord your God, to keep all His statutes and His commandments, which I command you and your son and your son's son, all the days of your life; and that your days may be prolonged.

Deut 6:2

THE NEW TESTAMENT

And He laid His hands on them and departed from there. Now behold one came and said to Him, "Good Teacher, what good thing shall I do that I may have eternal life?" So He said to him, "Why do you call Me good? No one is good but One, that is God. But if you want to enter into life, keep the commandments.

Matt 19:15-17

This is the message which we have heard from Him and declare to you, that God is light and in Him is no darkness at all.

John 1:5

For it is the God who commanded light to shine out of darkness, who has shone in our hearts to give the light of the knowledge of the glory of God in the face of Jesus Christ.

II Cor 4:6

THE QURAN

And in their footsteps We sent Jesus, the son of Mary, confirming the law that had come before him. We sent him the Gospel. Therein was guidance and light and confirmation of the law that had come before him, a guidance and an admonition to those who fear God.

5:49

O Prophet (Muhammad)! Truly We have sent you as a witness, a bearer of glad tidings and a warner.

33:45

CHAPTER 3
CHARACTERISTICS OF MESSENGERS AND PROPHETS OF GOD

Peace and salutation to Noah among the nations!
Say: God speaks the Truth: follow the religion of Abraham, the
sane in faith; he was not of the pagans.
—[Quran 3:95]—

Peace and salutation to Abraham!
–[Quran 36:109]—

Moses: he was specially chosen,
and he was an apostle and a prophet.
Peace and salutation to Moses and Aaron!
–[Quran 37:120]—

Peace and salutation to such as Elias (Elijah).
–[Quran 37:130]—

To Jesus the son of Mary, We gave clear (signs),
And strengthened him with the holy spirit.
–[Quran 2:253]—

Jesus said, so peace (salutation)
is on me, the day I was born, the day I die, and the day that I
shall be raised up to life again (resurrection)
–[Quran 19:33]—

We sent thee not (O Muhammad) but as a Mercy
for all creatures.
–[Quran 21:107]—

CHAPTER 3
CHARACTERISTICS OF MESSENGERS AND PROPHETS OF GOD

All the messengers of God (may the peace and blessings of God be upon them) exemplify God's religion by their states of certainty, security and total commitment. On them are showered the blessings of the Almighty. They have been addressed in the scriptures with the honored titles of messengers, prophets, truthful, trustworthy, sincere, unadulterated, pious, and guides. Now it has been the consistent tragedy of the human intellect, either unenlightened or mischievously misled by their satanic enemy, to invoke "lack of relevance, understanding and applicability" of the revelation to their human affairs. That is why, in the grand scheme of things, the Almighty had made the exemplifying messengers as essential models of His revelational guidance. There is no better explanation of any idea, however abstract, when one sees a human phenomenon that stands as its formal and behavioral manifestation. This is precisely why in the primary declarations of His religion, the acceptance and submission to His will by the exemplifying messengers have been made essential. All the blessed messengers across the scale of time and the vastness of the earth have invited their people towards God's religion. They would be the first ones in the unblemished state of submission and be perfect living models of obedience to God's commandments, in all and the minutest aspects of their conduct. All the messengers from God to humankind carried the same divine message. Their invitation was to the affirmation of the same, one and only God, His guidance, His grand design of here and the hereafter, and the path of unconditional and unadulterated submission to His commandments as the universal prescription for felicity in this life and salvation in the other.

The blessed messenger Noah, while inviting his people to God, asserted that he himself has been ordered by God to enter in complete submission to His Will (*islam*). Prophet Abraham was invited by the Almighty to accept His will (*islam*), which he did, and in his will and testament to his sons, including Prophet Jacob, he revealed to them that the Almighty has chosen for them the ways of submission to their Creator (*islam*) and he wishes that they would not die except in the state of obedience to the Almighty (*islam*).

This covenant was repeated by Prophet Jacob in his last days. The reward for Prophet Abraham's sincerity and purity in the way of total submission, without the slightest deviation, was that God declared him to be His friend, a guide to all nations, and promised guidance and stations of honor to his progeny. When Prophet Moses spoke to his people, he too invited them to declare their belief in God, and put their trust as subservient to God and thus become Muslims. The disciples of Prophet Jesus identified themselves as believers in submission to His will (*muslim*s).

And finally, in one verse after another, as the Quranic guidance is pronounced to mankind and for all time to come, through Prophet Mohammed, the way of Islam is repeatedly pointed out as resonant with and a continuation and completion of the previous divine messages. With the revelation of the Quran, the divine guidance was unambiguously established as was done in the Torah, Gospels and Psalms. The truth has always appeared in its resolute brilliance while falsehood is often reduced to a flimsy fog. The characteristics that distinguished the state of God's religion from the state of doubt and denial, were clearly introduced in the scriptures. The arrogant doubters of the Almighty and the deniers of His perennial religion were disheartened. It has been prophesied by God, the Master of All Time, that in their final hours, all deniers will lament and wish that they too had accepted and followed the way of total submission to His divine message. Prophethood is thus the manifestation of God's benevolence to guide human beings to their destination, the kingdom of God, the eternal life in heaven.

There were prophets in all nations preaching the same religion of One God in the respective languages of those nations. Some names are mentioned in the holy scriptures while some are not.

The Quran mentions only the twenty-five most prominent prophets by name. They are: Adam, Noah, Hud, Salih, Abraham, Enoch, Ishmael, Isaac, Lot, Jacob, Joseph, Shuaib, Job, Moses, Aaron, Ezekial, David, Solomon, Elias, Elisha, Jonah, Zachariah, John the Baptist, Jesus, and Muhammad. All are blessed, deserving salutation from the universe.

In the light of verses of the Quran, A. Yusuf Ali describes the characteristics of some prophets:

> The great exemplars of virtue conquered evil, each according to his circumstances: Abraham stood staunch in the fire of persecution, unhurt; Lot was bold in reproving abominations; Noah survived the flood by his faith, in a world of unbelief; David sought justice, and sang God's praises; Solomon by wisdom subdued the refractory; Job was patient in suffering; Ishmael, Idris, and Zul-kifl were true in constancy amid temptation; Jonah turned to God after a short misunderstanding; Zakariah and his family were exemplars of devoutness and Mary of chastity. All men and women of God form one united brotherhood.[1]

All the chosen messengers, bestowed with the divine message, are the sublime beams of One light. They are fundamentally, inherently and essentially of the same material. Their unique significance is the feeling of complete obedience in the presence of God in every aspect of their lives. They are all sacred, free of sins and faults. They are symbols of His mercy and grace in this world. They guide humanity like a sacramental guiding light in the dark vastness of time. The leaders of the travelers on the straight path carry a banner of infinite beauty and perfection of the Almighty's truth. They set examples of worshiping God by demonstrating in their deeds out of sheer love of God, not out of hope for reward or punishment. This is the most exalted state of spiritual ascension. They perceive themselves as mirrors in which the unique beauty of God and some of His attributes are reflected. They are walking on this earth with the kingdom of heavens in their sleeves.

They guide human beings heavenward. They understand the architectural plan of this heaven, the astounding manifestation of His power to create. With humbleness and great latitude of tolerance for neglect and ridicule, they walk amongst the disbelievers with awful splendor and humbleness. Their mission is to enlighten lives of the human beings with love, compassion and grace from God. In fact, they are a benign link between man and the Creator, as God speaks with mankind through them. God's grace did not ask for any price for the essentials to sustain physical life of human beings on this earth. The air, sun, fresh water, and the elements are free. Similarly, the divine guidance had to be free for spiritual life. The prophets also did not seek or expect any reward from men for preaching and delivering the divine message. On the contrary, they all bear lots of sufferings at the hands of unthankful and unfortunate human beings, puffed up with false pride and malice of ignorance. They did not disagree with each other. They have testified that each one has brought eternal Truth that has been revealed to them by God at various time intervals. Prophet Jesus said, "Think not that I am come to destroy the law of the prophets: I have not come to destroy, but to fulfill."[2]

The divine message brought by the prophets was rejected by the rich, arrogant leaders of that nation and the community. The majority followed those proud leaders instead of accepting the divine revelations. The prophets were threatened and persecuted because they identified in the arrogant leaders vices of hypocrisy and worldliness, drenched with sins of every kind.

They preached to study the laws of nature and thus subjugate the physical world by obeying those laws. This would create harmonious relationships amongst His creation with ultimate benefits to all forms of life. They proclaim equality amongst rich and poor, black and white and all human beings. The only ones dear to the Almighty are the pious amongst human beings. They preached unconditional submission to His laws and decrees. The values which worldliness admires like greed and selfishness were condemned by them. Their message is to enlighten the spirit with righteousness and self-enrichment through sacrifice, charity and love. Their mission is to place humanity on the shining straight path of Truth. They feel pain watching humanity wrapped in absolute moral darkness. They cry seeing human beings drowning in superstition, cruelty, and sins.

Their mission is to convert barren lands of immorality into a blooming garden of hope, morality, love, and righteousness. They introduce the Almighty, All-loving, Most Merciful Creator of the universe to human beings. They are the fountains flowing into the streams of eternal Truth, providing hope and salvation for mankind. They ask every human being to serve God, by obeying His laws in all the affairs of life with humbleness, devotion, and reverence. In spite of the fact that the world turns against them and persecutes them, they perform their missions with enthusiasm, love, compassion, and unparalleled zeal. They accept no compromise. No one can dare conquer their sublime courage. There is not an infinitesimal amount of fear of any threats of worldly powers, of consequences of annoying the self claimed leaders of a community decaying in the depths of spiritual and moral corruption. They demand and command the uprising of human beings against any kind of tyranny and injustice of false leaders and rulers.

In their preaching, no person has a right to claim exclusive privileges due to socioeconomic status. They break down the barriers of caste, creed and color. Without formal education in any school or institution recognized and accredited by worldly standards, they appeal to reason, awaken faculties of intellect; persuade acquisition of knowledge; induce the human mind towards the scientific study of nature and its implications for human benefit. Their life is a personification of righteousness, thus they teach the highest spiritual values. They awaken human conscience and direct her to obedience of God's Laws in human affairs. They invite men to repentance and direct them to seek and beg for forgiveness from the most merciful God, because they are the bearers of the glad tidings of the mercy of God. They do not speak for any personal motives in the worldly sense. They say anything only when Almighty God commands them to say. A. Yusuf Ali, in the light of verses from the Quran, narrates the story of Moses:

> God's Messengers are men and win through good life by God's grace and their faith. So Moses was saved from the tyrant's wrath in infancy, and reared in the tyrant's own den, but gently in a mother's love. In youth was he endowed with wisdom and knowledge, strength and the will to do right. In sorrow of misfortune he trusted in God and opened his heart to Him. In self-imposed exile he won love by his chivalry and confidence in the Truth. In his mission he triumphed over arrogant wrong by his meekness, patience, and faith. So good follows good and evil must fall, cursed, loathed, disgraced, and despised.[3]

A. Yusuf Ali describes the story and mission of Moses, as mentioned in verses of the Quran:

> The story of how Moses was chosen and told of his

mission, has a high mystic meaning. He was true to
his family and solicitous for their welfare. Encamped
in the desert, he saw a fire far off. Approaching, he
found it was holy ground. God did reveal Himself to
him, so that he saw life in things lifeless, and the light
in his glorified Hand, that shone white with light
divine. Armed with these Signs he was told to go forth
on his mission. But he thought of his brother Aaron,
and prayed that God might join him in his mission,
and his prayer was granted.[4]

God describes special status and characteristic miracles of
Prophet Jesus in the Quran:

> *Then will God say: O Jesus, the son of Mary!*
> *Recount My favor to you and to your mother. Behold! I*
> *strengthened you with the holy spirit, so that you did*
> *speak to the people in childhood and in maturity.*
> *Behold! I taught you the Book and Wisdom, the Law*
> *and the Gospel and behold! you made out of clay, as it*
> *were, the figure of a bird, by My leave, and you*
> *breathed into it, and it becomes a bird by My leave, and*
> *you heal those born blind, and the lepers, by My leave.*
> *and behold! you bring forth the dead by My leave. and*
> *behold! I did restrain the Children of Israel from (vio-*
> *lence to) you when you did show them the Clear Signs,*
> *and the unbelievers among them said: 'This is nothing*
> *but evident magic.'*
> *And behold! I inspired the disciples to have faith in*
> *Me and My Messenger They said, 'We have faith, and*
> *do you bear witness that we bow to God as Muslims'."*[5]

In the Quran God mentions the miraculous birth of Prophet
Jesus and his special characteristics as a prophet, teaching His
commandments in childhood and maturity:

> *Behold! the angels said: "O Mary! God gives you*
> *glad tidings of a Word from Him: his name will be*
> *Christ Jesus, the son of Mary, held in honor in this*
> *world and the Hereafter and of (the company of) those*

nearest to God; He shall speak to the people in child-
hood and in maturity and he shall be (of the company)
of the righteous. She said: "O my Lord! how shall I
have a son when no man has touched me?"

He said: "Even so: God created what He will. When
He has decreed a Plan, He but says to it, 'Be,' and it is!
And God will teach him the Book and Wisdom, the
Law and the Gospel,[6]

An anonymous but saintly person describes the impact of
Prophet Jesus on the annals of humanity,

ONE SOLITARY LIFE

He was born in an obscure village. He worked in a
carpenter shop until he was thirty. He then became an
itinerant preacher. He never held an office. He never
had a family or owned a house. He didn't go to college.
He had no credentials but himself. He was only thirty-
three when the public turned against him. His friends
ran away. He was turned over to his enemies and went
through the mockery of a trial. . . . All the armies that
ever marched, all the navies that ever sailed, all the
parliaments that ever sat, and all the kings that ever
reigned have not affected the life of a man on this
earth as much as that one solitary life.[7]

Ameer Ali describes Prophet Muhammad,

At the dawn of the 7th century of the Christian
era, in the streets of Mecca might often be seen a quiet
thoughtful man, past the meridian of life, his Arab
mantle thrown across his shoulders, his tailasan
drawn low over his face; sometimes gently sauntering,
sometimes hurrying along, heedless of the passers-by,
heedless of the gay scenes around him, deeply
absorbed in his own thoughts—yet withal never for-
getful to return the salutation of the lowliest, or to
speak a kindly word to the children who loved to
throng around him. This is al-Amin, "the
Trustworthy." He has so honorably and industriously
walked through life, that he had won for himself from

his compatriots the noble designation of the true and trusty.[8]

We have seen this wonderful man as an orphan child who had never known a father's love, bereft in early childhood of a mother's care, his early life so full of pathos, growing up from a thoughtful childhood to a still more thoughtful youth. His youth as pure and true as his boyhood; his manhood as austere and devout as his youth. His ear ever open to the sorrows and sufferings of the weak and the poor; his heart ever full of sympathy and tenderness towards all God's creatures. He walks so humbly and so purely, that men turn round and point, there goes 'al-Amin', the true, the upright, the trusty. A faithful friend, a devoted husband; a thinker intent of the mysteries of life and death, on the responsibilities of human actions, the end and aim of human existence—he sets himself to the task of reclaiming and reforming a nation, nay, a world, with only one loving heart to comfort and solace him. Baffled, he never falters; beaten, he never despairs. He struggles on with indomitable spirit to achieve the work assigned to him. His purity and nobleness of character, his intense and earnest belief in God's mercy, bring round him ultimately many a devoted heart; and when the moment of the severest trial comes, like the faithful mariner, he remains steadfast at his post until all his followers are safe, and then betakes himself to the hospitable shore: such we have seen him. We shall see him now the king of men, the ruler of human hearts, chief, lawyer, and supreme magistrate, and yet without any self-exaltation, lowly and humble. His history henceforth is merged in the history of the commonwealth of which he was the center. Henceforth the preacher who with his own hands mended his clothes, and often went without bread, was mightier than the mightiest sovereigns of the earth.[9]

VERSES ON CHARACTERISTICS OF MESSENGERS AND PROPHETS OF GOD

THE QURAN

Do they seek for other than the religion of God?—while all creatures in the heavens and on earth have, willing or unwilling, bowed to His will (accepted *islam*), and to Him shall they all be brought back.

3:83

We sent not a Messenger except (to teach) in the language of his (own) people, in order to make (things) clear to them. Now God leaves straying those whom He pleases and guides whom He pleases: and He is exalted in Power, full of Wisdom.

14:4

And this was the legacy that Abraham left to his sons and so did Jacob, "O my sons! God has chosen the faith for you; then die not except in the faith of islam."

2:132

Moses said, "O my people! If you do (really) believe in God, then in Him put your trust if you submit (your will to His)."
They said, "In God do we put our trust."

10:84-85

THE QURAN

And behold! I inspired the disciples to have faith in Me and My Messenger. They said, "We have faith and do bear witness that we bow to God as Muslims."

4:115

The Messenger believed in what had been revealed to him from his Lord as do the people of faith. Each one (of them) believes in God, His angels, His books and His apostles. "We make no distinction (they say) between one and another of His Messengers." And they say, "We hear and we obey. (We seek) Your forgiveness, Our Lord, and to You is the end of all journeys.

2:285

Say: "We believe in God, and in what has been revealed to us and what was revealed to Abraham, Ismail, Isaac, Jacob, and the tribes, and in (the Books) given to Moses, Jesus and the prophets from their Lord. We make no distinction between one and another among them and to God do we bow our will (in Islam)."

3:84

THE QURAN

O mankind! there has come to you a direction from your Lord and a healing for the (diseases) in your hearts, and for those who believe, a guidance and a mercy.

10:57

It is He Who sent down to you (O Muhammad) (step by step) in truth the Book, confirming what went before it and He sent down the law (of Moses) and the Gospel (of Jesus) before this, as a guide to mankind, and He sent down the Criterion (of judgment between right and wrong).

3:3

We have, without a doubt, send down the Message and We will assuredly guard it (from corruption).

15:9

Nay more, it is for us to explain it (and make it clear).

70:17, 19

PART II
PROCESS

CHAPTER 4
COMMANDMENTS:
GOD'S WILL BE DONE

The precepts of the Lord are right,
rejoicing the heart;
the commandment of the Lord is pure,
enlightening the eyes.
–PSA 19:9–

No one is good but One, that is God.
But if you want to enter into life,
keep the commandments.
–Matt 19:17–

God commands justice,
doing of good, and liberality
to relatives,
and He forbids all shameful deeds
and injustice and rebellion.
He instructs you that you may receive an admonition.
–[Quran 16:90]–

Verily you are ordered the divine commandments,
then forsake them not.
–Prophet Muhammad—

CHAPTER 4
COMMANDMENTS:
GOD'S WILL BE DONE

The human mind is in awe in imagining the magnificent power of the divine command, "Be!" that resulted in this miraculous existence. The human spirit stands in perpetual wonder at the abject obedience of this preexistent nothingness that ordered itself into this precise, complex, colorful, dynamic, and law-abiding universe of spirit and matter in dimensions beyond human comprehension. Ever since the human being arrived at this stage of existence it has been driven by this wonder to find the inner and outer limits of this universe to gaze at its horizons and to understand the intricacies of its workings. Every effort forces awe. It is estimated that the age of the universe is no less than twenty billion years.

This vast universe is in a state of perfect obedience towards its Creator because each element has an assigned purpose. A commandment, when executed without malice, becomes its evident destiny. This fact of creation is a sign for the human being to grasp the essence of total obedience. Human beings have to accept their Creator as the supreme sovereign, the ultimate focus of all praise, the only source of all guidance, worthy of complete obedience, and the ultimate judge of all right and wrong. They recognize the purpose of creation through the wisdom of the divine commandments, through the acceptance of the patterns of conduct as established by the messengers, and to obey the Creator through His messengers with free will, with sincerity and without compromise.

The universality of the religion revealed by God is evident, like a shining sun, in the commandments as the divine Truth. The first and foremost commandment is to accept the kingship of the Most Merciful and the Most Compassionate Creator of the universe. His supreme sovereignty deserves and demands that only He is worthy of issuing commandments. And it is the utmost, unreserved, and undivided duty of human beings to obey those commandments without any alteration, digression and deflection. This obedience with firm faith, sincerity of purpose and with earnest desires and efforts is expressed in deeds. Human beings are bestowed with wisdom to understand the benefits of obeying those commandments. The glittering sign of His mercy and grace is that those commandments have never changed with the change of time, geographical boundaries or with different languages. The consistency, the congruity, the vitality and the permanence in the nature and objectives of these commandments are based on one radiating purpose. And it is to create a spiritually healthy human society, void of doom, gloom, destruction, and eventual annihilation.

Once a human being has accepted from the bottom of his/her heart with logic and understanding the sovereignty of One God, then the other commandments pertain to interpersonal relationships, accepted or rejected behaviors, distinctions between right and wrong, demarcations between moral and immoral, definitions of virtue and depravity, guidance for piety, and identification and avoidance of routes plunging into the dark gorges of sin.

A. Yusuf Ali, in light of verses from the Holy Quran, described:

> The good men and true, who succeeded Abraham,
> received the gifts of revelation and guidance, and kept
> alive God's Message, which now is proclaimed in the

Quran in which is blessing and confirmation of all that
went before. In the daily pageants of nature—the
dawn and the restful night, the sun, the moon, the
stars that guide the mariner in distant seas, the rain-
clouds pouring abundance, and the fruits that
delight the heart of man—can you not read signs of
God? No vision can comprehend Him, yet He knows
and comprehends all.[1]

The physical universe is in on the pattern of accepting and
obeying His laws. Such is its created nature. This pattern is
universally applicable to all that is between the heavens and
the earth. They are all in a state of unqualified submission to
the divine scheme which is analogous to the extreme prostration of the created towards the Creator. They have all been
instructed and well rehearsed in their "rituals of affirmation,"
of their role in the grand scheme. They do not disobey and they
do not deviate even the slightest, and thus they are all in the
state of unconditional submission.

Human beings are offered this pattern as divine mercy, but
this had to be adopted by choice and with free will. Only the
human being has the distinction to willingly enter the state of
obedience and thus not only wins freedom from the fears and
anxieties of existence but also wins the rewards of the hereafter.
Exile from obedience condemns human beings to the punishments of the hereafter.

A. Yusuf Ali emphasizes the sincere devotion to Almighty
God in the light of verses from the Holy Quran:

> To God is due sincere devotion, and to Him alone:
> there is none like unto Him. All nature obeys His laws,
> and our own growth and life proclaim Him Lord and
> Cherisher. How can we blaspheme? We must serve
> Him, the One, the True, with sincere devotion, and fol-
> low His Law in its highest meaning: or else the loss is
> our own. All nature proclaims aloud His grace and lov-
> ing-kindness.[2]

If faith is the affirmation of the human's station before His Creator, then obedience is the lived-out manifestation of that station. If religion (faith) is the commitment, deeds are the expressions of that commitment. If faith is the declaration that there is no god worthy of submission and adoration of the human except the One and Unique Almighty God, then morality in deeds is the manifested life of the submission and adoration.

Obedience is evidenced in deeds like a slave of the Almighty, sincerely, consciously, willfully, exclusively, without any malice or malcontent, without any compromise or adulteration, and without selfish desires would perform the assigned task. It is the honored station attainable by the human beings. To surrender one's being to the "slavery" of the Almighty is a guarantee of protection from the enslavement of the human being by other gods, predators of the human mind and soul. So fundamental is the recognition and establishment of this relationship that it had been declared by the Almighty as the sole purpose of the creation of the human being.

A. Yusuf Ali presents a rational view for submission to His Will in the light of Quranic verses,

> God is all-in-all: follow His Law and His Light, and obey His messenger, who invites you to deeds of goodness and charity. Strive and spend your resources yourselves in the cause of God: He will grant you a light to go before you and guide you to your eternal goal, where no evil can enter. When success crowns your efforts, even then is the time to humble yourselves before God, on sincere witness to His love. The pleasures here below are deceptive: be foremost in seeking God and His good pleasure: trust Him: be not like those who mistook mere renunciation of the world for God's service. God's grace is for all: be your love and your service for all.[3]

While the being of the Almighty is unfathomable by the human mind, the state of total obedience, however, is understandable and a possible pattern of religious life for an individual as well as for members of the society. While it is impossible for the human being to analyze the Almighty, it is possible, and has been considered desirable and necessary to honor the station of submission to His commandments. Furthermore, it is in the bounteous and unselfish gifts of nature that the human beings are invited to see the glory, beneficence, and mercy of his Creator in Whose slavery they may attain the fulfillment of the purpose of their creation.

The protocol of this obedience is to simultaneously obey the Almighty and His appointed and blessed messengers. And those who attain this station of allegiance and persevere in it are honored and admitted into the sphere of His bounties, wherein are included the apostles, the truthful and the martyrs. It is possible only if a person demonstrates the required obedience by honest and sincere deeds. God's religion is the straight way which leads to the state of harmony among the various dimensions of the individual and collective existence. As the human mind is enlightened by the cognition of this submission, as the soul is refined by the discipline of obedience, as the doubts of the mind start to evaporate and as the soul progresses towards the state of certainty about the unseen, the individual starts to enter the domain of perfect subservience, the state of security, certainty, and absolute faith. Those who arrive at the state of perfect obedience, heaven attests their trust in God and His chosen way for them.

Those who obey the commandments of the Almighty are real fortunate ones, the honored, the peaceful, and the contented. Their Creator is pleased with them and they also are in a state of blissful peace with their supreme Lord. Repeatedly, God keeps inviting, instructing, and commanding His human creation to obey Him and His messengers, to open their minds and souls to His revelations and to structure their lives according to His laws.

The divine scheme for humans beings has become abundantly clear. The mercy of the Creator has engulfed humankind in all epochs of history, in the form of His guidance, in compact, precise, and simple language of their own time, exemplified by the blessed messengers and guides who were from among themselves. One can say with faith that the word used for this guidance, this divinely gifted code for life, which is *islam* in the Arabic language of the Quran, would have been the corresponding identical word in other languages. Humankind is perpetually blessed with the commandments to do the "honorable" and not the disallowed." These commandments are homogeneous to the created nature of human beings and they are the agents that cause the corresponding effects on the individual and collective life of human society.

What are these commandments? None other than the sincere love towards fellow human beings; sharing of pains in sorrows and participation in the benign joyous matters; caring for the orphans and widows, the destitute, the abandoned and those fallen in the way of misery and sickness; helpful concern for the neighbors, a guiding hand and shelter for the wayfarer; feeding of the hungry; standing up for the tyrannized; speaking up for the oppressed; fulfilling the promises; acquisition and transmission of knowledge; and steadfastness in the pursuit of the Truth. These are the life giving seeds from which will spring forth the all-season garden of a loving and caring society. These are the essential building blocks for the house of peace in this world and an eternal edifice of felicity in the hereafter.

VERSES ON COMMANDMENTS: GOD'S WILL BE DONE

THE OLD TESTAMENT

My commandments shall you keep and My statutes shall you keep to walk therein. I am the Lord your God. You shall therefore keep My statutes and My ordinances which if a person does, he shall live by them. I am the Lord.

Lev 18:4, 5

Sow to yourselves according to righteousness; reap according to mercy; break up your fallow ground for it is time to seek the Lord until He come and cause righteousness to rain upon you.

Hos 10:12

And rend your heart and not your garments and turn unto the Lord your God for He is gracious and compassionate, long-suffering and abundant in mercy, and repents him of the evil.

Joel 2:13

Judge the poor and fatherless. Do justice to the afflicted and destitute. Rescue the poor and needy. Deliver them out of the hand of the wicked.

PSA 82:3, 4

I am the Lord your God Who brought you out of the land of Egypt. And you shall observe all My statues and all My ordinances and do them. I am the Lord,

Lev 19:36, 37

THE NEW TESTAMENT

Submit yourselves therefore to God.

Jas 4:7

We ought to obey God rather than men.

Acts 5:29

Lead a quiet and peaceable life in all godliness and honesty.

I Tim 2:2

Follow after righteousness, godliness, faith, love, patience, meekness.

I Tim 6:11

Add to your faith virtue and to virtue, knowledge, and to knowledge, temperance, and to temperance, patience, and to patience, godliness, and to godliness, brotherly kindness, and to brotherly kindness, charity.

II Pet 1:5-7

Love your enemies. Bless them that curse you. Do good to them that hate you. Pray for they who despitefully use you and persecute you.

Matt 5:44

Children, obey your parents in the Lord for this is right. Honor your father and mother which is the first commandment with promise.

Eph 6:1-2

THE QURAN

Say: "What has come to me by inspiration is that Your God is One God. Will you therefore bow to His Will (in *islam*)?"

21:108

And obey God and the Messenger that you may obtain mercy.

3:132

O you who believe! Fear God and be with those who are true (in word and deed).

9:119

And be steadfast in prayer. Practice regular charity. Bow down your heads with those who bow down (in worship).

2:43

Who is he that will loan to God a beautiful loan which God will double unto his credit and multiply many times? It is God that gives (you) want or plenty and to Him shall be your return.

2:245

Give full measure when you measure and weigh with a balance that is straight. That is the most fitting and the most advantageous in the final determination.

17:35

Your Lord has decreed that you worship none but Him and that you be kind to parents.

17:23

SAYINGS ON COMMANDMENTS: GOD'S WILL BE DONE

My Lord has commanded me nine things: (1) To reverence Him, externally and internally; (2) to speak the truth, and with propriety, in prosperity and adversity (3) moderation in affluence and poverty; (4) to benefit my relations and kindred, who do not benefit me; (5) to give alms to him who refuse me; (6) to forgive him who injure me; (7) that my silence should be in attaining a knowledge of God; (8) that when I look on Gods creatures, it should be as an example for them: and God has ordered me to direct in that which is lawful.

"What is Islam?" someone asked. Muhammad said, "Purity of speech and charity."

No man is true in the truest sense of the word but he who is true in word, in deed, and in thought.

Strive always to excel in virtue and truth.
Traditions of Prophet Muhammad

In every aspect of life submit yourself to your Creator's Will (commandments) with sincerity, devotion and enthusiasm.
Ali ibn Abi Talib

One shall speak truth.
Laws of Manu

Be fearless and pure. Never waver in your determination or your dedication to the spiritual life. Give freely. Be self-controlled, sincere, truthful, loving, and full of the desire to serve. Realize the truth of the scriptures; learn to be detached and to take joy in renunciation. Do not get angry or harm any living creature, but be compassionate and gentle; show good will to all. Cultivate vigor, patience, will, purity; avoid malice and pride. Then, Arjuna, you will achieve your divine destiny.

To be steadfast in self-sacrifice, self-discipline, and giving in sat. To act in accordance with these three is sat as well. But to engage in sacrifice, self-discipline, and giving without good faith is asat, without worth or goodness, either in this life or in the next.

Strive constantly to serve the welfare of the world. By devotion to selfless work one attains the supreme goal of life. Do your work with the welfare of others always in mind. It was by such work that Janaka attained perfection. Others, too, have followed this path.

Bhagavad Gita

They who know the truth are not equal to those who love it, and they who love it are not equal to those who delight in it.

Absolute Truth is indestructible. Being indestructible, it is eternal.

Hold faithfulness and sincerity as first principles.

In view of gain, he thinks of righteousness; in view of danger, he is ready to sacrifice his life; in addition, he never forgets his promise, however far back; such a person may also be considered a perfect person.

Base character on righteousness, conduct according to propriety expressed in modesty, and become complete in sincerity.

Confucius

Do good to him who has done you an injury.

Lao Tzu

Just as treasures are uncovered from the earth, so virtue appears from good deeds, and wisdom appears from a pure and peaceful mind. To walk safely through the maze of human life, one needs the light of wisdom and the guidance of virtue.

Right View, Right Thought, Right Speech, Right Behavior, Right Livelihood, Right Effort, Right Mindfulness and Right Concentration. This is called the Truth of the Noble Path to the Cessation of the Cause of Suffering.

Abide pure amid the impurities of the world; thus shall you find the way of religion.

Buddha

Let your body be chaste, virginal, clean,
Let faith in God be the staff on which you lean;
Let brotherhood with every man on earth
Be the highest aspiration of your Yogic Order.
Know that to subdue the mind
Is to subdue the world.
Hail, all hail unto Him,
Let your greetings be to the Primal God;
Pure and without beginning, changeless,
The same from age to age.
Let knowledge of God be your food,
Let mercy keep your store,
And listen to the Divine Music
That beats in every heart.

To abide by Your will, O formless One, is the human being's best offering; You who are eternal, abiding in Your peace.

Guru Nanak

CHAPTER 5
COMMANDMENTS:
YOU SHALL...

Wisdom/Knowledge
Morality
Prayer-Worship
Patience-Perseverance
Courtesy
Mercy-Forgiveness
Charity
Defense of Righteousness (*jihad*)
Fasting
God-wariness

CHAPTER 5
COMMANDMENTS: YOU SHALL . . .

WISDOM/KNOWLEDGE

T he awakening of the human soul is exhibited by creeping rays of wisdom on the horizon of mind. The enlightened mind and soul accept the glorious faith in the divine message. Once a person establishes a firm faith that everything has its purpose, is beneficial, dutiful and genuine, that faith opens gateways which leads to higher levels of perennial wisdom. Every prophet has emphasized to man that he must tread the paths to wisdom and to avoid those leading to dead, dark alleys of ignorance, pride and prejudice. Wisdom propagates alignment of healthy thoughts. It produces social and logical concordance. It promotes a harmonious relationship amongst beneficial deeds. It is the foundation of God's laws. It is the basis of noble virtues. It is the explanation and justification of difference between good and evil. It enlightens the intellectual faculty to foresee the consequences of doing good and avoidance of evils.

Wisdom blended with pragmatic instructions, promoting compassion and loving kindness guarantees happiness and peace. The balance of mind is a gift from wisdom which measures every conceptual and perceptual reality facing a human mind.

It has been mentioned in the Scriptures that no person is

born evil. It is the lack of wisdom, bankruptcy in harmonious relationship with the divine laws and the stupidity of falling in the traps of satan that leads towards vices of ignorance, evil and darkness of the human soul. The well established fact is that wisdom blossoms into happiness by virtuous deeds. There is a logic in calling wisdom a real wealth which cannot be stolen or robbed. Through wisdom, prudence, insight, self-control, and governing of the impulses, the human mind plans and implements virtuous thoughts into action for his/her salvation and welfare of the human society.

Verses on Wisdom/Knowledge

The Old Testament

Buy the truth and sell it not. Also wisdom, instruction and understanding.
Pro. 23:23

Hear counsel and receive instruction that you may be wise in your latter end.
Prov 19:20

How much better is to get wisdom than gold! Yea, to get understanding is rather to be chosen than silver.
Prov 16:16

The fear of the Lord is the beginning of wisdom and the knowledge of the All-holy is understanding.
Prov 9:10

Teach me good discernment and knowledge for I have believed in Your commandments.
PSA 119:66

The New Testament

Walk circumspectly not as a fool, but as wise.
Eph 5:15

Who is wise and understanding among you? Let him show by good conduct that his words are done in the meekness of wisdom.
Jas 3:13

The wisdom that is from above is first pure, then peaceable, gentle and easy to be intreated.
Jas 3:17

But the wisdom that is from above is first pure, then peaceable, gentle, willing to yield, full of mercy and good fruits, without partiality and without hypocrisy.
Jas 3:17

The Quran

He grants wisdom to whom He pleases and he to whom wisdom is granted receives indeed a benefit overflowing, but none will grasp the message but men of understanding.
2:269

Know that God gives life to the earth after its death! Already have We shown the signs plainly to you that you may learn wisdom.
57:17

My Lord! Grant me increase in knowledge.
20:114

For the worst of beasts in the sight of God are the deaf and the dumb—those who understand not.
8:22

SAYINGS ON WISDOM/KNOWLEDGE

Seek knowledge from the cradle to the grave.

Acquire knowledge. It enables its possessor to distinguish right from wrong; it lights the way to heaven; it is our friend in the desert, our society in solitude, our companion when friendless; it guides us to happiness.

One hour's meditation on the work of the Creator is better than seventy years of prayer.

To spend more time in learning is better than spending more time in praying; the support of religion is abstinence. It is better to teach knowledge one hour in the night than to pray the whole night.

Who are the learned? They who practice what they know.
Traditions of Prophet Muhammad

Belief and wisdom are twin brothers; God accepts not the one without the other.

There is no treasure like knowledge.

The realm of knowledge has no bounds.

The chief of the talents is knowledge.

Knowledge leads to wisdom; accordingly the educated man is the wise one.

Riches diminish by expenditure, while knowledge is increased by dissemination.

That knowledge is very superficial which remains only on

your tongue; the intrinsic merit and value of knowledge is that you act upon it.

Ali ibn Abi Talib

One who is endowed with Self-Knowledge loves all beings.

The knower of the Self overcomes grief and delusion.

By knowing God one is released from all fetters.

When one has faith, then he thinks. One who lacks faith does not think.

Upanishad

The man unknowing and without faith, his soul full of doubt, perishes.

Even if you were the most sinful of sinners, Arjuna, you could cross beyond all sin by the raft of spiritual wisdom. As the heat of a fire reduces wood to ashes, the fire of knowledge burns to ashes all kama. Nothing in this world purifies like spiritual wisdom.

Those who take wisdom as their highest goal, whose faith is deep and whose senses are trained, attain wisdom quickly and enter into perfect peace. But the ignorant, indecisive lacking in faith, waste their lives. They can never be happy in this world or any other.

There is no purifier in this world equal to wisdom.

To be wise, you should be modest, sincere, gentle forbearing, just. You should venerate your spiritual guide and be pure, steadfast, self-controlled. Cultivate knowledge pertaining to the self and a view to the meaning of reality. All this together constitutes wisdom. What deviates from this is ignorance.

The Bhagavad Gita

The Master said, "Learn as though you would never be able to master it; hold it as though you would be in fear of losing it."

The Master said, "In education there is no class distinction."

Confucius

He who knows others is learned; he who knows himself is wise.

Lao Tzu

As a solid rock is not shaken by the wind, wise people falter not amidst blame and praise.

Faith, modesty, humbleness, endeavor and wisdom are the great sources of strength to him who is seeking enlightenment. Among these, wisdom is the greatest of all and the rest are but the aspects of wisdom.

If a man's faith is unsteady, if he does not know the true law, if his only peace of mind is troubled, his knowledge will never be perfect.

Buddha

My system began
With the beginning of the breath of life.
Its source is the wisdom of the True Guru
The True Guru is the Word,
And intensive consciousness is the disciple.

Guru Nanak

MORALITY

The Most Merciful and the Most Compassionate has the most noble intentions, functions and benefaction for the happiness of mankind. A divine spark in the human soul, a living conscience, instills virtues for goodness, prosperity and salvation of mankind. This spark can be kept kindling and the virtues, moral excellence, can be kept blooming only through obedience to the will of God. The faculty to judge between 'good' and evil is a divine gift of God, a natural blessedness, a universal grace, uniquely bestowed in human intellect. This natural and universal ability of judgment contains seeds of virtue which keep the conscience in everlasting blooming stage of a perfumed garden.

The beauty and the nobility in the moral laws is that these are God's commandments, Who is the most Intelligent, All-knowing, and the most benevolent. These moral laws, components of His commandments, are never changing. Man has not been assigned by the Creator with any authority to make or unmake the moral laws. Any attempt to do that has resulted in destruction of civilizations.

It is essential for human intelligence to understand that morality serves a purpose in this world. It fulfills the need, the objective and the design of human creation. Morality is the hope and means of human existence. The laws rule and guide the human behavior. They are essentials for the moral health of a human society.

The conscience engineers the human behavior in general. It warns that all wrongs must be avoided and that all evil must be crushed. This rationalistic combination of cause and effect into a higher stage of truth is trustworthy and unerring. This glorious flame, ignited by divine spark, is imperishable and ever burning.

PRAYER/WORSHIP

Worship is a comprehensive word. One cannot call it prayer because it is much more than just any ritualistic prayer or a supplication. It is not just a confession of one's transgressions and a plea for divine mercy. Neither can one call it a ritual worship, because it is not a ritual in the usual sense of the word, and because worship implies an object of worship and that the Almighty is beyond the imaginations of time and place, of size and shape. Worship is in fact a renewal, a disciplined affirmation, of the believer's station of obedience before his Creator, thanksgiving for the divine message and the messengers and declaration that a person seeks the example of the divinely appointed exemplifier, and also seeks the divine protection from the seductions of satan and his companions, the true enemies of mankind. Worship is a self- discipline of mind, soul, and actions. A spiritual act demands its conception in the mind by wisdom and spark of divine lights. It is flourished by prayers and is complete when accepted by the God through His grace. Worship is the divinely prescribed act of remembrance that will never let the soul forget nor the mind reject, nor the body overrule, the original covenant, "Verily we testify that You are our God: the Sustainer, the Cherisher. We obey only Your commands and nobody else: Your will be done," always.

In the light of the verses of the Holy Quran, A. Yusuf Ali describes worship:

> There is nothing secret in our world or in creation, which does not depend ultimately on God's will and plan. Every affair goes back to Him for a decision. Therefore we must worship Him and trust Him. Worship implies many things: (1) trying to understand His nature and His will; (2) realizing His goodness and glory, and His working in us as a means to this end; (3) keeping Him in constant remembrance and celebrating His praise, to whom all praise is due; and (4) completely identifying our will with His, which means obedience to His law and service to Him and His creatures in all sincerity.[1]

There are components of worship of God. There are pillars on which a building stands firmly; foundations which do not let the strong 'satanic' winds shake it. Human beings stare at His creation in heaven and earth with reverence and wonder. They admire the Creator, Cherisher and Provider within limits of their intellectual levels. The admiration and adoration of the creatures leads them to heartfelt prostration, admiration, and appreciation of the Creator, Almighty One God.

The self- realization awakens in hearts. The realization and acceptance of the purpose of creation appears like a shinning light on the horizon of knowledge, a gift of the Creator. A tide of burning desire to submit and obey washes away the satanic barricades and they admit, profess, and humbly a vow, "We obey Your will: Laws and Commandments. In doing so, we seek Your guidance and help."

They understand that this acknowledgment, a pledge of obeying His commandment, is not confined to 'lip service.' It relates to deeds. It is manifested in purity of thoughts and sincerity in actions. This submissive admiration by establishing a covenant with the Creator demands a demonstrated proof of subservience in every plan , scheme, step and stage of its implementation in daily life.

Realizing and understanding the limitations and weaknesses of human faculties and capacities, one humbly and earnestly seeks and begs for His grace and guidance leading to the straight way, illustrated for those whom God has bestowed with His grace, those loved and blessed ones who are showered by His rewards. They became models and symbols of His love and grace for humanity.

Awareness about the arch enemy of human beings and comprehending satan's malicious intentions, his disruptive and destructive powers, his mean abilities to sabotage human beings, they beg and seek God's help and protection from wandering away from the straight way. They ask His guidance to avoid treading on the crooked path of the unfortunate ones who earned wrath of God by walking into the paths of satanic temptations which are condemned by God and His messengers.

VERSES ON PRAYER/WORSHIP

THE OLD TESTAMENT

You shall make your prayer unto Him and He will hear you and you shall pay your vows.
Job 22:27

Give ear, O Lord, unto my prayer and attend unto the voice of my supplications.
PSA 86:6

As for me, I will call upon God and the Lord will save me. Evening and morning and at noonday will I complain and moan and He has heard my voice.
PSA 55:17, 18

For He has satisfied the longing soul and the hungry soul He has filled with good.
PSA 107:9

Make me to hear joy and gladness; that the bones which You have crushed may rejoice. Hide Your face from my sins and blot out all mine iniquities. Create me a clean, heart O God and renew a steadfast spirit within me. Cast me not away from Your presence and take not Your holy spirit from me.
PSA 51:10-13

THE NEW TESTAMENT

You shall worship the Lord your God and unto him only shall you serve.
Luke 4:8

Why sleep? Rise and pray lest you enter into temptation.
Luke 22:46

Is any among you afflicted? Let him pray.
Jas 5:13

Ask and it shall be given to you. Seek and you shall find. Knock and it shall be opened unto you.
Matt 7:7

Whatsoever we ask, we receive of Him because we keep His commandments and do those things that are pleasing in His sight.
John 3:22

Continue in prayer and watch in the same with thanksgiving.
Col 4:2

Pray for one another.
Jas 5:16

THE QURAN

Say: "O my Lord! Let my entry be by the gate of Truth and honor and likewise my exist by the gate of Truth and honor and grant me from Your Presence an authority to aid (me)."
17:80

To those whose hearts, when God is mentioned, are filled with fear, who show patient perseverance over their afflictions, keep up regular prayer and spend (in charity) out of what We have bestowed upon the;m.
22:35

Be sure we shall test you with something of fear and hunger, some loss in goods or lives or the fruits of your toil but give glad tidings to those who patiently persevere. Who say when afflicted with calamity, "To God We belong and to Him is our return." They are those on whom (descend) blessings from God and mercy and they are the ones that receive guidance.
2:155-157

VERSES ON PRAYER/WORSHIP

THE OLD TESTAMENT

Heal me, O Lord, and I shall be healed. Save me and I shall be saved for You are my praise.

Jer 17:14

Remove from me the way of falsehood. Grant me Your law graciously. I have chosen the way of faithfulness. Your commandments have I set (before me). I cleave unto Your testimonies. O Lord, put me not to shame.

PSA 119:29-31

I will give thanks unto You with uprightness of heart when I learn Your righteous commandments. I will observe Your statutes. O forsake me not utterly.

PSA 119:7-8

God is our refuge and strength, a very present help in trouble.

PSA 46:1

THE NEW TESTAMENT

When you pray, you shall not be as the hypocrites are for they love to pray standing in the synagogues and in the corners of the streets that they may be seen of men.

Matt 6:5

In this manner, therefore, pray: "Our father in heaven, hallowed be Your name. Your kingdom come. Your will be done on earth as it is in heaven. Give us this day our daily bread and forgive us our debts as we forgive our debtors. Lead us not into temptation, but deliver us from evil for Yours in the kingdom and the power and the glory forever. Amen."

Matt 6:9-13

I exhort therefore that, first of all, supplication, prayers, intercessions and giving of thanks be made for all men.

I Tim 2:1

Ask in faith nothing wavering.

Jas 1:6

The effectual fervent prayer of a righteous man avails much.

Jas 5:16

Rejoicing in hope, patient in tribulation, continuing steadfastly in prayer.

Rom 12:12

THE QURAN

On no soul does God place a burden greater than it can bear. It gets every good that it earns and it suffers every ill that it earns. (Pray:) "Our Lord! Condemn us not if we forget or fall into error. Our Lord! Lay not on us a burden like that which You laid on those before us. Our Lord! Lay not on us a burden greater than we have the strength to bear. Blot out our sins. Grant us forgiveness. Have mercy on us. You are our Protector. Help us against those who stand against faith."

2:286

SAYINGS ON PRAYER/WORSHIP

The Lord does not regard a prayer in which the heart does not accompany the body.

He whom prayer prevents not from wrongdoing and evil, increases in nothing save in remoteness from the Lord.

O Lord, I supplicate You for firmness in faith and inclination towards the straight path, and for Your aid in being grateful to You, and in adoring You in every good way; and I supplicate You for an innocent heart which shall not incline to wickedness and for a true tongue. I supplicate You to guide me from all which You know to be virtuous and to preserve me from all which You know to be vicious. I supplicate You to forgive me my faults for You know them all.

Prayer is the *miraj* (union with or annihilation in the divine essence by means of continual upward progress) of the faithful.
Traditions of Prophet Muhammad

Prayers remove sinful desires from your mind as strong wind sheds dried leaves from trees. It frees you from the clutches of vice and wickedness.

No worship or prayer are more sacred than fulfillment of obligation and duties in the path of righteousness.
Ali ibn Abi Talib

May we know the Lord of lords, the King of kings, the God of gods; God, the God of love, the Lord of all.

I go for refuge to God who is ONE in the silence of eternity, pure radiance of beauty and perfection, in whom we find our peace. He is the bridge supreme which leads to immortality, and the spirit of fire which burns the dross of lower life.

Om, may Brahman protect us both (the preceptor and the disciple)! May Brahman bestow upon us both the fruit of knowledge! May we both obtain the energy to acquire knowledge! May what we both study reveal the Truth! May we cherish no ill feeling toward each other! Om. Peace! Peace! Peace!

Upanishad

Only through praise and prayer to God mind will become pure.

He shall become pure, whosoever repeats His Name with devotion, affection and heartfelt love.

Without praise of the Almighty, darkness shalt prevail in one's mind. The first and the foremost name of God is clearly depicted as 'Sat' (Eternal Truth) which shows the ever existence of God:

O Companion, O Formless, O Bodiless, Prop of all;
O World-Creator, O Treasure of attributes, in Your court there is always justice.
O Incomprehensible, Destroyer of sins, most remote You are, was, and shall be
O Constant Companion of saints, Support of without support.
O Lord! I am Thy servant, I am without virtue, I have no merit;
Saith Nanak, grant me the gift of Your Nam that I may engrave it in my heart.

Guru Nanak

PATIENCE/PERSEVERANCE

Once the gateway to enlightenment of the human soul is opened by the gift of wisdom; once the faith in God is deeply rooted in the human mind; once a sincere, keen, desire to obey the real Master, Sovereign King of kings, overwhelms all other desires; once a covenant is established between the Creator, Cherisher, Sustainer and the human slave and subservient; once an unbinding urge springs from the bottom of the human being's heart to bow, prostrate and pray to Almighty God for guidance, love, grace, and mercy; once a blessed person starts treading on the path of righteousness after conquering the voracious passions; and once the virtuous efforts crown the fortunate persons with the grace of God, the Sovereign King, then the person enters the realm of true and sincere believer.

The blessed human beings, striving to walk on the 'straight path of righteousness' in the footprints of holy people, seek Almighty God's help, love, guidance, grace, and mercy through prayers and virtuous deeds. They remain steadfast with patience, perseverance, constancy, and self-restraint. They refuse to be allured and intimidated by their enemy, satan. The highest reward for patience and restraining from fear, anger, and passions is that Almighty God guarantees His support.

The steadfastness on the straight way in the face of all kinds of opposition from evil forces, hardships, and afflictions is an assurance from the Most Powerful for His blessings. God confirms His support. He promises the promotion to ascension to heaven. Bearing all difficulties, adversities, and afflictions in the cause of justice and truth; subduing all mischievous impulses, controlling malign passions and carnal desires are confirmed guarantees for progress toward God.

VERSES ON PATIENCE/PERSEVERANCE

THE OLD TESTAMENT

The Lord is righteous in all His ways and gracious in all His works. The Lord is nigh unto all them that call upon Him, to all that call upon Him in truth. He will fulfill the desire of them that fear Him; He also will hear their cry and will save them. The Lord preserves all them that love Him, but all the wicked will He destroy.

PSA 145:17-20

With my whole heart have I sought You. O let me not err from Your commandments. Your Word have I laid up in my heart that I might not sin against You. Blessed are You, O Lord. Teach me Your statutes.

PSA 119:10-12

When He has regarded the prayer of the destitute and has not despised their prayer.

PSA 102:18

THE NEW TESTAMENT

Take, my brethren, the prophets who have spoken in the name of the Lord for an example of suffering, affliction and of patience. Behold we count them happy which endure. You have heard of the patience of Job and have seen the end of the Lord that the Lord is very pitiful and of tender mercy.

Jas 5:10-11

Giving all diligence, add to your faith virtue and to virtue, knowledge and to knowledge, temperance, and to temperance, patience, and to patience, godliness.

II Pet 1:5, 6

Rejoicing in hope, patient in tribulation, continuing steadfastly in prayer.

Rom 12:12

Watch you in all things, endure afflictions.

II Tim 4:5

Be not slothful, but followers of them who through faith and patience inherit the promises.

Heb 6:12

THE QURAN

O you who believe! Seek help with patient perseverance and prayer for God is with those who patiently persevere.

2:153

Say: "Truly my prayer and my service of sacrifice, my life and my death, are all for God, the cherisher of the worlds. No partner has He. This am I commanded and I am the first of those who bow to His will."

6:162-163

To those whose hearts when God is mentioned are filled with fear, who show patient perseverance over their afflictions, keep up regular prayer and spend (in charity) out of what We have bestowed upon them.

22:35

"Our Lord," they say, "Let not our hearts deviate now after You have guided us, but grant us mercy from Your own Presence for You are the Grantor of bounties without measure."

3:8

SAYINGS ON PATIENCE/PERSEVERANCE

The key of paradise is prayer, and the key of prayer is ablution.

When the Messenger of God entered a place of worship he said, "O God! pardon my sins, and open for me the gates of Your compassion"; and on leaving he would repeat the same.

O Lord, grant to me the love of You; grant that I love those that love You; grant that I may do the deeds that win Your love; make Your love dearer to me than self, family and wealth.

Be persistent in good actions.
Patience is half of faith.
Traditions of Prophet Muhammad

Acquire patience and endurance, because their relation with true faith is that of a head to a body; a body is of no use without a head, similarly true faith can be of no use without attributes of resignation, endurance and patience.

Affliction is easily borne by one who knows how to be patient.
Ali ibn Abi Talib

Should various misfortunes assail you, persevere in patience of body, speech, and mind.
Buddha

COURTESY

Strong and steadfast faith in God, sincere determination and dauntless efforts to obey His commands are the foundations supporting a structural and formational relationship between human beings and Creator. This steady, stable, and unshakable bond creates, cultivates and nourishes some unique characteristics in the human behavior.

Sober and deep mental commitment illuminate the truth that His commandments are directed towards interpersonal relationships to establish a friendly society under the shadow of divine grace. The observance of daily life under His commandments reveals one fact that humans are created for the well-being of other humans. The contentment, happiness, and enlightenment are guaranteed through deeds of courteousness, respect, love, sympathy, generosity, compassion, and kindness. To honor social responsibilities with these glorious attributes is fulfillment of the objectives of human creation. This is true worship. The universality of God's religion inspires human soul with a sublime respect for morality. It commands and encourages every thought, every act, and every behavior which fosters respect, love, and affection between members of human society and condemns everything that creates anguish, agony, grief and harshness amongst human beings. A. Yusuf Ali has highlighted in footnotes of the verses in the Holy Quran:

> (1) Even to your enemies and the enemies of God you should speak fair: who are you to judge others? Judgment belongs to God alone, for He knows you best, and your personal knowledge is at best imperfect. And Satan is always trying to divide mankind. (2) Amongst yourselves also you should not entertain suspicions, but speak politely according to the best standards of speech. A false or unkind word may destroy all your efforts at building up unity, because the forces of disruption are more numerous than the forces of unity.[2]

You foil hatred with love. You repel ignorance with knowledge, folly and wickedness with friendly message of Revelation. The man who was in the bondage of sin, you not only liberate him from sin, but make him your greatest friend and helper in the cause of God! Such is the alchemy of the Word of God![3]

Spotless purity in thought, word, and deed, includes the disposition to put the best construction on the motives so that we ascribe no evil motive to the seeming indiscretions of virtuous people. Such high standard can only be by the grace of God, Who hears all prayers and knows all the temptations to which human nature is subject. His Will and Plan make both for spiritual protection and spiritual peace, and we must place ourselves trustingly in his hands.[4]

VERSES ON COURTESY

THE OLD TESTAMENT

I command you, saying, "You shall surely open your hand to the poor and needy brother in your land.
Deut 15:11

It had been told you, O human being, what is good and what the Lord does require of you: only to do justly and to love mercy and to walk humbly with your God.
Mic 6:8

You shall not take vengeance nor bear any grudge against the children of your people but you shall love your neighbor as yourself: I am the Lord.
Lev 19:18

THE NEW TESTAMENT

Be you all of one mind having compassion one of another, love as brethren, be pitiful, be courteous.
I Pet 3:8

Be of one mind, live in peace and the God of love and peace shall be with you.
II Cor 13:11

If a man say, "I love God," and hates his brother, he is a liar.
John 4:20

First cast out the beam out of your own eye and then shall you see clearly to cast out the mote out of your brother's eye.
Matt 7:5

THE QURAN

The believers are but a single brotherhood: So make peace and reconciliation between your two (contending) brothers and fear God that you may receive mercy.
49:10

Serve God and join not any partners with Him and do good—to parents, kinsfolk, orphans, those in need, neighbors who are near, neighbors who are strangers, the Companion by your side, the wayfarer (you meet), and what your right hand possesses for God loves not the arrogant, the vainglorious.
4:36

VERSES ON COURTESY

THE OLD TESTAMENT

It is the discretion of a man to be slow to anger and it is his glory to pass over a transgression.
> Prov 19:11

A soft answer turns away wrath but a grievous word stirs up anger.
> Prov 16:7

Learn to do well. Seek justice, relieve the oppressed, judge the fatherless, plead for the widow.
> Isa 1:17

These are the things that you shall do: Speak you every man the truth with his neighbor; execute the judgment of truth and peace in your gates; and let none of you devise evil in your hearts against his neighbor; and love no false oath; for all these things that I hate say the Lord.
> II Ech 8:16

Behold how good and how pleasant it is for brethren to dwell together in unity!
> PSA 133:1

THE NEW TESTAMENT

Murmur not among yourselves.
> John 6:43

Be patient towards all people.
> I Thess 5:14

Speak evil of no man.
> Tit 3:2

Honor all men.
> I Pet 2:17

Children, obey your parents in the Lord for this is right. Honor your father and mother which is the first commandment with promise that it may be well with you and you may live long on the earth.
> Eph 6:1-3

But I say to you, "Love your enemies; bless those who curse you; do good to those who hate you; and pray for those who spitefully use you and persecute you."
> Matt 5:44

Owe no person anything, but to love one another.
> Rom 13:8

Judge not according to appearances, but judge righteous judgment.
> John 7:24

He that is without sin among you, let him cast the first stone.
> John 8:7

THE QURAN

When a (courteous) greeting is offered you, meet it with a greeting still more courteous or (at least) of equal courtesy. God takes careful account of all things.
> 4:86

Nor can goodness and evil be equal. Repel (evil) with what is better. Then will he be between whom and you was hatred become as it were your friend and intimate!
> 61:34

O you who believe! Let not some men among you laugh at others it may be that the (latter) are better than the (former): nor let some woman laugh at others: it may be that the (latter) are better than the (former): nor defame nor be sarcastic to each other, nor call each other by (offensive) nicknames: ill-seeming is a name connoting wickedness (to be used of one) after he has believed: and those who do not desist are (indeed) doing wrong.
> 49:11

SAYINGS ON COURTESY

To do unto all men as you would wish to have done unto you, and to reject for others what you would reject for yourself.

Who is the most favored of God? He from whom the greatest good comes to His creatures.

Whoever is not grateful to man is never grateful to God.

No father has given his child anything better than good manners.

He who wishes to enter Paradise at the best door must please his father and mother.

Heaven lies at the feet of mothers.

He is the most perfect Muslim whose disposition is best and the best of you are they who behave best to their wives.

When the bier of anyone passes by you, whether Jew, Christian, or Muslim, rise to thy feet.

True modesty is the source of all virtues.

Humility and courtesy are acts of piety.

You will not enter paradise until you have faith, and you will not complete your faith until you love one another.

Do you love your Creator? Love your fellow-beings first.

Verily God instructs me to be humble and lowly and not proud; and that no one should oppress another.

What actions are most excellent? To gladden the heart of a

human being, to feed the hungry, to help the afflicted, to lighten the sorrow of the sorrowful, and to remove the wrongs of the injured.

Shall I not inform you of a better act than fasting, alms, and prayers? Making peace between one another: enmity and malice tear up heavenly rewards by the roots.

It is not worthy of a speaker of truth to curse people.

Verily the most beloved of you by me, and nearest to me in the next world, are those of good dispositions; and verily the greatest enemies to me and the farthest from me, are the ill-tempered.

Assist any person oppressed, whether Muslim or non-Muslim.

It was said to the Prophet, "O Messenger of God! Curse the infidels." Muhammad said, "I am not sent for this; nor was I sent but as a mercy to mankind."

Give the laborer his wage before his perspiration be dry.
Traditions of Prophet Muhammad

The most detestable man is he who returns evil for good, and the most praiseworthy, he whose answer to villainy is a generous deed.

Whoever is not serviceable to his kind is to be counted among the dead.

Hide the good you do, and make known the good done to you.

There is no adornment like politeness.

Treat another as you would yourself.

Put away vindictiveness, and you will have tranquility of mind and heart.

Ali ibn Abi Talib

To speak without irritating others, words that are true, pleasing, and beneficial, and to recite and study sacred texts-that is austerity in speech.

To be austere in mind means inner peace and joy, a kind of disposition, stillness, self-control, and purifying one's place in the world.

The ignorant work for their own profit, Arjuna; the wise work for the welfare of the world, without thought for themselves. Perform all work carefully, guided by compassion.

The Bhagavad Gita

In their ethics, they espouse self-reliance, self-realization and spontaneous behavior, but always within the context of a larger whole of society and nature.

Master said, "It is, in private life, to be courteous; in business, to be attentive; in all human relations, to be honest. And it should never be abandoned, even though one goes to live amid the barbaric tribes of the east or north."

Do not do to others what you do not want done to yourself.

A man who exacts much from himself and little from others will certainly avoid resentment.

The Master said, "Grieve not that men do not know you; grieve that you do not know men."

Confucius

Whoever, by good deed, covers the evil done, such a one illumines the world like the moon freed from clouds.

Faith removes greed, fear and pride; it teaches courtesy and to respect others; it frees one from the bondage of circumstances; it gives one courage to meet hardship; it gives one power to overcome temptations; it enables one to keep one's deeds bright and pure; and it enriches the mind with wisdom.

He who wishes his own happiness by causing pain to others is not released from hatred, being himself entangled in the tangles of hatred.

Let a man overcome anger by love, let him overcome evil by good; let him overcome the greedy by liberality, the liar by truth!

Buddha

The man who knows God looks on all men as equal, as the wind blows on the commoner and the king alike.

Guru Nanak

MERCY/FORGIVENESS

It is a universally acknowledged fact, substantiated by the history of humanity that human weaknesses are the stumbling blocks in the straight way delineated by God. The archenemy, satan, and his companions are planning and designing to lay down every hurdle on the straight path. They create every kind of hindrance in the path of human salvation.

The most astonishing fact is that they manipulate the human intelligence to justify the illicit deeds in the minds of persons who are under the influence of satan and are committed to immoral deeds. This miserable condition of the human mind, shadowed by satanic influence, stumbling, wavering, and faltering false heartedly, persuades persons to commit sins. God, the Creator of human beings, knows these weaknesses, the vulnerability of the human mind and the agony of an inflicted soul. The most outstanding attributes of God, our Cherisher as well as our Creator, All-knowing about our shortcomings and rebellions, are His mercy, His forgiveness and His grace. The illness, sufferings and torture of human souls may be sins, mistakes, blunders, or evil intentions.

God can and will embrace them with His forgiveness and mercy if there is a sincere repentance and heartfelt cry for mercy and forgiveness arising from the depths of anguished souls. The sincere repentance is revival and rejuvenation of a covenant to heal the conduct, to give up attitudes of disobedience, rebellion, and to turn back on the righteous path of submission and subservience to His will. It is another way of expressing one's gratitude in acceptance and recognition of His grace and benevolent power of forgiveness. Even a person with living conscience can tumble over and fall into the ditches of sin or error. The divine revelations give a message not to moan or despair. The sinner is guided to ask for forgiveness of the Most Merciful God. The faith of that person lights up hope. The guiding hand pulls him/her out of the darkness of wrong conduct and puts that person on the enlightened path of righteousness.

It is further emphasized in a footnote by A. Yusuf Ali on the verse of the Holy Quran,

> Even hypocrites can obtain forgiveness, on four conditions: (1) sincere repentance, which purifies their mind; (2) amendment of their conduct, which purifies their outer life; (3) steadfastness and devotion to God, which strengthens their faith and protects them from the assaults of evil; and (4) sincerity in their religion, or their whole inner being, which brings them as full members into the goodly Fellowship of Faith.[5]

The verses in the Old Testaments, New Testament, The Quran are quoted in the Table. God's mercy and forgiveness are infinite. The only hope for a striving human to spiritually survive and thrive in this world and to ascertain ascension to immortality in life after death is through His mercy, forgiveness and grace.

VERSES ON MERCY/FORGIVENESS

THE OLD TESTAMENT

O give thanks unto the Lord of lords for His mercy endures forever. To Him who alone does great wonders, for His mercy endures forever. To Him that by understanding made the heavens for His mercy endures forever.
PSA 136:3-5

But the mercy of the Lord is from everlasting to everlasting upon them that fear Him and His righteousness unto children's children; to such as keep His covenant and to those that remember His precepts to do them.
PSA 103:17-18

THE NEW TESTAMENT

But God, Who is rich in mercy, because of His great love with which He loved us.
Eph 2:4

You shall know the truth and the truth shall make you free.
John 8:32

He shall have judgment without mercy that has shown no mercy.
Jas 2:13

Blessed are the merciful for they shall obtain mercy.
Matt 5:7

THE QURAN

So say, "O my Lord! Grant forgiveness and mercy for You are the best of those who show mercy.
23:118

Be you foremost (in seeking) forgiveness from your Lord and a garden (of bliss), the width whereof is as the width of heaven and earth, prepared for those who believe in God and His Messenger. That is the grace of God which He bestows on whom He pleases and God is the Lord of grace abounding.
57:21

VERSES ON MERCY/FORGIVENESS

THE OLD TESTAMENT

But if the wicked turn from all his sins that he has committed and keeps all My statues and does that which is lawful and right, he shall surely live, he shall not die.
Ezek 18:21

It has been told to you, O human being, what is good and what the Lord does require of you only to do justly and to love mercy and to walk humbly with your God.
Mic 6:8

But the Lord, the God of hosts, the Lord is His name. Therefore turn you to your God. Keep mercy and justice and wait for your God continually.
Hos 12:6-7

Let not kindness and truth forsake you. Bind them about your neck. Write them upon the table of your heart.
Prov 3:3

Happy is he whose transgression is forgiven, whose sin is pardoned.
PSA 32:1

THE NEW TESTAMENT

But go and learn what this means: I desire mercy and not sacrifice for I did not come to call the righteous but sinners to repentance.
Matt 9:13

For if you forgive people their trespasses, your heavenly father will also forgive you, but if you do not forgive people their trespasses, neither will your Father forgive your trespass.
Matt 6:14-15

Judge not and you shall not be judged. condemn not and you shall not be condemned. Forgive and you shall be forgiven.
Luke 6:37

Repent therefore and be converted that your sins may be blotted out.
Acts 3:19

Bless them which persecute you. Bless and curse not.
Rom 12:14

THE QURAN

Moses prayed, "O my Lord! Forgive me and my brother! Admit us to Your mercy for You are the Most Merciful of those who show mercy.
7:151

Say, "O my servants who have transgressed against their souls! Despair not of the mercy of God for God forgives all sins for He is Oft-forgiving, Most Merciful."
39:53

The evil one threatens you with poverty and bids you to conduct unseemly. God promises you His forgiveness and bounties and God cares for all and He knows all things.
2:268

Know they not that God does accept repentance from His votaries and receive their gifts of charity and that God is verily He, the Oft-returning, Most Merciful.
9:104

But verily your Lord—to those who do wrong in ignorance but who thereafter repent and make amends, Your Lord, after all this, is Oft-forgiving, Most Merciful.
16:119

SAYINGS ON MERCY/FORGIVENESS

God is not merciful to him who is not so to mankind.

All-Merciful has mercy upon the merciful people. Have mercy upon the earthly creatures that the One who is in the heaven have mercy on you.

Verily you have two qualities which God and His messenger love—fortitude and gentleness.

That person is nearest to God, who pardons, when he has power over him who would have injured him.

Verily those who are patient in adversity and forgive wrongs, are the doers of excellence.

He does not belong to us who does not show mercy to our young ones and respect to our old ones; who does not recommend what is reputable and prohibit what is disreputable.

Traditions of Prophet Muhammad

Never lose hope and confidence in the mercy of God.

The penitent finds his way back to God.

Forgiveness is the crown of great qualities.

Ali ibn Abi Talib

Compassion is not merely for fellow human beings, but for all creatures;

Lao Tzu

Compassion is no attribute. It is the Law of Laws. . . a shoreless universal essence, the light of everlasting right and fitness of all things, the law of love eternal.

Buddha

He that would know His height, must be of the same height;

only the Lord knows the greatness of the Lord. Saith Nanak, only be God's grace and bounty are God's gifts bestowed on man.

Salvation comes only through His Grace. O Nanak, this alone need we know, that God, being Truth, is the one Light of all.

On the imperfect who repent O Nanak, God bestows virtue, on the striving virtuous, He bestows increasing blessedness.

Priceless His mercy and priceless His will. Those who try to express it are mute in adoration.

Guru Nanak

CHARITY

The obedience to His commandment, "Love human beings," is best manifested in acts of charity. The significance of the righteous deed, charity, is an example of the domination of the spirit in human life. The constitution and the fundamentals of charity are faith and love. The greatest benefactor of human beings provides for the health, harmony and welfare of a human society and thus He linked charity as a commandment with a command to worship. Its association with worship implicates a wide range and variety of deeds in charity. It is much more than giving a percentage of your income. It embodies, in addition to money or material goods, all the advantages, faculties, speciality in various fields of knowledge or science to share and to place at the service of others who are in need of these.

Prophet Muhammad said, "In fact, every unselfish good act is a charity." The motivation in these virtuous acts of charity is a keen and sincere desire for the countenance of obedience to His will and seeking only the pleasure and approval of God. It is not doing any favor to another person, or expecting rewards or compensation. Control and self sacrifice mean purification of soul and its spiritualization.

Those who treated this world to be an ethical arena, who shared their fortunes with the less fortunate, who spread their earnings among those who could not earn, who shunned the temptations to become possessive and exclusive about their abilities, who shared their knowledge with the less knowledgeable, who lent their eyes to the blind, who became legs for those who could not walk, who became scribes for those who could not write, who founded institutions for human welfare, who left charities that would not cease with their life, who gathered beneficial knowledge and made it available to others, who gave themselves and their property with generosity, with unselfishness, as gratitude to the Almighty Who Gave them in abundance . . . such have been hailed by the revelations as, "The ones who have extended their Lord a beautiful loan," that He may return it manifolds, in this world and in the other. In light of the verses in the Quran, A. Yusuf Ali describes charity:

Three questions arise in charity: (1) What shall we give? (2) To whom shall we give? and (3) How shall we give? The answer is: Give anything that is good, useful, valuable. It may be property or money; it may be a helping hand; it may be advice; it may be a kind word; "whatever you do that is good" is charity. On the other hand, if you throw away what is useless, there is no charity in it. Or if you give something with a harmful intent, eg., a sword to a madman, or a drug or sweets or even money to some one whom you want to entrap or corrupt, it is no charity but a gift of damnation. To whom should you give? It may be tempting to earn the world's praise by a gift that will be talked about, but are you meeting the needs of those who have the first claim on you? If you are not, you are like a person who defrauds creditors: it is no charity. Every gift is judged by its unselfish character: the degree of need or claim is a factor which you should consider. If you disregard it, there is something selfish behind it. How should it be given: As in the sight of God. This shuts out all pretense, show, and insecurity.[6]

False charity "to be seen of men," is really no charity. It is worse, for it betokens a disbelief in God and the Hereafter. "God sees well whatever ye do." It is compared to a hard barren rock on which by chance has fallen a little soil. Good rain, which renders fertile soil more fruitful, washes away the little soil which this rock had, and exposes its nakedness. What good can hypocrites derive even from the little wealth they may have amassed?[7]

Our Charity of Love is called a loan to God, which not only increases our credit account manifold, but obtains for us the forgiveness of our sins, and the capacity for increased service in the future.[8]

Giving to the needy has been repeatedly emphasized in the Old Testament, New Testament, and Quran. S. Ameer Ali has quoted a saying from Prophet Muhammad defining charity. His definition of charity embraced a wide circle of kindness:

Every good act is charity. Your smiling at your

brother is charity; an exhortation addressed to your fellow human being to do virtuous deeds is equal to alms-giving. Putting a wanderer on the right path is charity; assisting the blind is charity; removing stones and thorns and other obstructions form the road is charity; giving water to the thirsty is charity. A man's true wealth hereafter is the good he does in this world to his fellow human beings. When he dies, people will ask, 'What property has he left behind him?' But the angels, who examine him in the grave, will ask, 'What good deeds have you sent before you?[9]

The above definition is a sublime image of God's commandment on charity.

VERSES ON CHARITY

THE OLD TESTAMENT

Happy is he that considers the poor. The Lord will deliver him on the day of evil. The Lord preserve him and keep him alive. Let him be called happy in the land and deliver him not unto the greed of his enemies.
PSA 41:2-3

The righteousness takes knowledge of the cause of the poor. The wicked understand not knowledge.
Prov 29:7

If your enemy be hungry, give him bread to eat. If he b e thirsty, give him water to drink.
Prov 25:21

He that is gracious unto the poor lends unto the Lord and He will repay unto him his good deed.
Prov 19:17

THE NEW TESTAMENT

And now abide faith, hope, charity, these three but the greatest of these is charity.
Cor 13:13

We should remember the poor.
Gal 2:10

Whoso has this world's good and sees his brother in need and shows no compassion, how does the love of God dwell in him?
John 3:17

Give alms of such things as you have.
Luke 11:41

The end of the commandment is charity out of a pure heart, of a good conscience and of faith unfeigned.
I Tim 1:5

THE QURAN

By no means shall you attain righteousness unless you give freely of that which you love and whatever you give of a truth, God knows it well.
3:92

They ask you what they should spend (in charity). Say: "Whatever you spend that is good is for parents and kindred and orphans and those in want and for wayfarers and whatever you do that is good, God knows it well.
2:215

For those who give in charity, men and women, and loan to God a beautiful loan, it shall be increased manifold (to their credit) and they shall have (besides) a liberal reward.
57:18

SAYINGS ON CHARITY

There are seven people whom God will draw under His own shadow, on the day when there will be no other shadow; one of them, a person who has given alms and concealed it, so that his left hand knew not what his right hand did.

Giving alms to the poor has the reward of one alms; but that given to kindred has two rewards; one, the reward of alms, the other, the reward of helping relations.

A giver of maintenance to widows and the poor is like a bestower in the way of God, an utterer of prayers all the night, and a keeper of constant fast.

Every good act is charity.

Traditions of Prophet Muhammad

Give to a poor man before he asks; for if you place him under the necessity of stretching out his hand, you take from his self-respect more than the value of your alms.

The best generosity is to forget the claim that you have against another, and to remember the right that someone has over you.

Ali ibn Abi Talib

Self-sacrifice, giving, and self-discipline should not be renounced, for they purify the thoughtful. Yet even these, Arjuna, should be performed without desire for selfish rewards. This is essential.

The sage does not hoard. Having bestowed all he has on others, he has yet more; having given all he has to others, he is richer still.

The Bhagavad Gita

To feed a person without loving him is to treat him like a pig. To love without respecting him is to treat him like a domestic pet.

Confucius

Charity is the universal love of all creation, not of a particular manifestation. He thus advocate a kind of ecocentric impartiality which results with identifying with the whole and which respects all beings as intrinsically valuable.

Lao Tzu

DEFENSE OF RIGHTEOUSNESS *(JIHAD)*

God's endowments to human beings are the divine messages to enlighten their souls. Human beings are duty bound to defend these glorious gifts as expression of heartfelt thanks and gratitude to God. The cunning and cruel enemy of human salvation is satan who has empowered himself with strong commitments to use all means and ways with malicious intentions for luring human beings who are striving and struggling to stay on the path of righteousness. The true defense is strong and solid faith in righteousness and perseverance in His cause laced with piety, justice and spiritual morality. Human beings are commanded to face and strive with full zeal against the assault of satan who uses evil thoughts, temptations, worldly benefits and lustful pleasures as his weapons. God has defined these human efforts as holy struggle, holy war and holy sacrifice.

The defense of faith in God's religion against the evil physical force laced with every kind of armor is commanded in His religion. Taking of arms and fighting are allowed only as a defensive measure against the onslaught of a force committed to destroy human society who is following God's commandments. It is also allowed to protect the innocent, helpless and tyrannized citizens under a despotic demon. Waging of war against any clan, any community or any country who extends the hands of peace toward followers of God's religion is forbidden by God. It is prohibited to use force to instill one's faith even if it may be religion of God. It is unlawful to attack and shed blood or intimidate by show of power force in extending the boundaries of a country or to influence or overshadow the faith of other people by using force with malicious influence. Acts of terrorism and killing of innocent people, children, women, and old folks are totally forbidden in One God's religion.

In the light of the verses of Holy Quran A. Yusuf Ali has described the defense of righteousness.

> The justification of righteousness in resisting oppression when not only they but their faith is persecuted and when they are led by a righteous Imam, is

that it is a form of self-sacrifice. They are not fighting for themselves, for land, power, or privilege. They are fighting for the right.[10]

War is only permissible in self-defense, and under well-defined limits. When undertaken, it must be pushed with vigor, but not relentlessly, but only to restore peace and freedom for the worship of God. In any case strict limits must not be transgressed: women, children, old and infirm men should not be molested, nor trees and crops cut down, nor peace withheld when the enemy comes to terms.[11]

VERSES ON DEFENSE OF RIGHTEOUSNESS

THE OLD TESTAMENT

When you go forth to battle against your enemies, see your enemies and see horses and chariots and a people more than you, you shall not be afraid of them for the Lord your God is with you who brought you up out of the land of Egypt. It shall be when you draw near unto the battle that the priest shall approach, speak unto the people and shall say to them: "Hear, O Israel, you draw near this day unto battle against your enemies. Let not your heart faint. Fear not nor be alarmed. Neither be afraid at them for the Lord your God is He that goes with you, to fight for you against your enemies and to save you."

Deut 20:1-4

When you go to war in your land against the adversary who oppresses you, sound an alarm with the trumpets.

Num 10:9

THE NEW TESTAMENT

Put on the whole armor of God that you may be able to stand against the wiles of the devil. For we do not wrestle against flesh and blood but against principalities, against power, against the rulers of the darkness of this age, against spiritual hosts of wickedness in the heavenly places. Therefore, take up the whole armor of God that you may be able to withstand in the evil day and having done all to stand. Stand therefore having girded your waist with truth, having put on the breastplate of righteousness and having shod your feet with the preparation of the gospel of peace. Above all, takin g the shield of faith with which you will be able to quench all the fiery darts of the wicked one. And take the helmet of salvation and the sword of the spirit which is the Word of God.

Eph 6:11-17

THE QURAN

To those against whom war is made, permission is given (to fight) because they are wronged and verily God is Mos Powerful for their aid. (They are) those who have been expelled from their homes in defiance of right (for no cause) except that they say, "Our Lord is God." Did not God check one set of people by means of another? There would surely have been pulled down monasteries, churches, synagogues, and mosques, in which the name of God is commemorated in abundant measure. God will certainly aid those who aid His (cause) for verily God is full of strength, exalted in might.

22:39-40

Fight in the cause of God those who fight you but do not transgress limits for God loves not transgressors.

2:190

SAYINGS ON DEFENSE OF RIGHTEOUSNESS

The most excellent *jihad* (holy war) is that for the conquest of self.

The best *jihad* is that a person speaks the truth before the tyrant ruler.

Prophet Muhammad saw a woman who had been killed in one of the battles, so he (the Holy Prophet) condemned the killing of women and that of the children.
Traditions of Prophet Muhammad

Never begin a war yourself, God does not like bloodshed, fight only in defense.

Never be first to attack your enemy, repulse his attacks, but do it boldly, bravely and courageously.

While declaring yourself and your deeds (*rajuz*, a custom amongst hand to hand combatants) never waste your time and instead of speaking about yourself speak about God and the Prophet.

Never follow and kill those who run away from the battle or an encounter, life is dear to them, let them live as long as death permits them to live.

Never kill wounded persons who cannot defend themselves.

Never strip naked a dead man for his coat of arms or dress.

Never take to loot or arson.

Never molest or outrage the modesty of a woman.

Never hurt a woman even if she swears at you or hurts you.

Never hurt a child.

Never hurt an old or an enfeebled person.

Ali ibn Abi Talib

Considering your dharman, you should not vacillate. For a warrior, nothing is higher than a war against evil. The warrior confronted with such a war should be pleased, Arjuna, for it comes an open gate to heaven. But if you do not participate in this battle against evil, you will incur sin, violating your dharma and your honor.

The Bhagavad Gita

FASTING

The straight path of righteousness leading to human salvation is vulnerable to highway robbery instigated by satanic thoughts. The basic instincts for food, drink, and sex are strong in our animal nature. Greed, lust and unscrupulous desires from the disturbed and destructive world place hurdles in the path of deliverance .

Any human being committed to step on this path needs to be equipped with faith, piety and discipline. Prayers, charity and virtues enable a person to ascend to higher levels of spirituality. Discipline controls the animal instincts and other worldly desires and places human thoughts and deeds in proper perspective. The exercise of self-restraint (fasting) is prescribed by God, to discipline in our behavior. The commandment of fasting is to restore harmony and balance between faith and deeds. Fasting provides an opportunity for spiritual elevation. It enriches the noble desire to submit to His will. It strengthens the human faculties of patience and steadfastness. It subdues animal passions, psychic cravings, lustful desires and thus cleanses the spirit from the pollution of carnal sins. It is also prescribed to observe the fast as expression of cognizance of wrong doing and then repenting for it.[12]

Alan Richardson has quoted the Old Testament describing fasting for repentance[13] or to be used as a kind of reinforcement for urgent supplication.[14] Imam Muslim has quoted in *Sahih Muslim*[15] Prophet Muhammad's saying,

> The best fasting in the eye of God is that of David, for he fasted for half of the age (he fasted on alternate days), and the best prayer in the eyes of God, the exalted and majestic, is that of David (peace be upon him), for he slept for half of the night and then stood for prayer and then again slept. He prayed for one-third of the night after midnight.[16]

The command to fast for the restoration of harmony and balance between faith and deeds has been addressed to the human race since its beginning. The attached table supports universality of the divine prescription for ailments of human souls.

VERSES ON FASTING

THE OLD TESTAMENT

Thus say the Lord of hosts: The fast of the fourth month and the fast of the fifth and the fast of the seventh and the fast of the tenth shall be to the house of Judah joy and gladness and cheerful seasons. Therefore love you truth and peace.

Zec 8:19

The hand of our God is upon all that that seek Him for good but His power and His wrath is against all them that forsake Him. So we fasted and besought our God for this and He was entreated of us.

Ezra 8:22-23

THE NEW TESTAMENT

Moreover when you fast, do not be like the hypocrites with a sad countenance for they disfigure their faces that they may appear to men to be fasting. Assuredly I say to you they have their reward. But you, when you fast, anoint your head and wash your face so that you do not appear to men to be fasting but to your Father who is in the secret place and your Father who sees in secret will reward you openly.

Matt 6:16, 17, 18

THE QURAN

O you who believe! Fasting is prescribed for you as it was prescribed to those before you that you may (learn) self-restraint.

2:183

SAYINGS ON FASTING

Fasting is an armor with which a man protects himself, so he (who fasts) should neither utter immodest speech nor act in an ignorant manner. If a man quarrels with him or uses derogatory words about him, he should say twice "I am fasting." And by Him in Whose charge is my life, the odor of the mouth of the fasting man in the estimation of God is sweeter than the odor of musk. "He gives up his food and drink and sexual desire for my sake. Fasting is for Me and I will grant him its reward; and a virtue brings reward ten times like it."

He who does not give up uttering falsehood and does not act according to what God has enjoined, God does not care for his giving up food and drink.

Traditions of Prophet Muhammad

The chief of the virtues is to curb the passions.

Ali ibn Abi Talib

The fasts are deemed by the Brahman as to be the essence of Tapas, the use of hunger to produce states of ecstasy is well attested.

The intellect is purified by self-control and concentration. When the intellect is purified, Atman shines forth.

Upanishad

If a man is trained in a discipline, becomes wholly purified, learns to control himself and his senses, his own individual existence now being the existence of all—even when he acts, he is not stained.

Thus the man of discipline, cleansed, constantly trained himself. He easily reaches God and tastes limitless joy.

But when a person wholly governing himself is roaming the sensual world with his senses under control, freed from likes and dislikes, he attains clarity.

The Bhagavad Gita

Make an island unto yourself. Strive without delay; fast; become wise. Purged of stain and passionless, you will not come again to birth and old age.

By sustained effort, earnestness, discipline, and self-control let the wise man make for himself an island which no flood overwhelms.

Buddha

GOD-WARINESS

Amongst the miracles of creation of human beings, the seat of human mind is the most awesome. Its structure, organization and harmonious relationships and interdependence amongst its parts create cosmic admiration for its Creator, the Almighty God. It seems that in this mass of neurons there are galaxies and constellations, sparkling, glimmering and flashing to reveal the handiwork of the most intelligent Creator.

Amongst the unbounded and fascinating duties assigned to the human brain by the Creator, the supreme duty is to understand, admire and nurture its abilities. The feelings of various colors, velocities and frequencies have a rippling effect on the human mind. It seems that the environment, experiences, memories, traditions and learnings are like throwing pebbles of different sizes and weights into a pond. Only the hand of divine guidance can supervise, control, and command the intensity of waves and the influence on human behavior. Only God's religion has provided answers to the enigma of life on this planet. Science has brought to light and explained the electrical and chemical mechanism by which the brain cells perform the assigned duties. Religion guides us as the human mind ascends to intellectual, spiritual and moral realizations and accomplishments.

Fear can cause anxiety of varying intensities or anxiety can produce fears of different constituents and combinations and strange foundations. This interlinked composition can have devastating effects on the human mind, subsequent thought processes and human behavior. The only way to eradicate the harmful affects of fear/anxiety is to seek the guidance and grace of God with the true fear of Him, lest we should diverge from His will, or do anything which would not be pleasing to Him. Prophet David has expressed God's Grace to shelter the fear in a psalm,

> *Oh, how great is Your goodness, which You have laid up for those who fear You, which You have pre-*

pared for those who trust in You in the presence of the sons of men![17]

Prophet Solomon has described the values of religious fear, the fear of the Lord is a fountain of life, to depart from the snares of death.[18]

God revealed His message in the Quran.

We send the apostles only to give good news and to warn: so those who believe and mend (their lives), - upon them shall be no fear, nor shall they grieve.[19]

The true fear of God is the foundation on which structure of wisdom stands. In the enlightened alleys of that structure conscience flourishes to attain high levels of morality. In this fear is an active assertion of a person's will not to disobey the Creator and Cherisher. It is also a faith and assurance in His grace and forgiveness.

In fact, the fear of God is seeded and kindred by love. Human beings should be afraid to disobey and to displease Him. The peace and contentment are guaranteed through sincere faith and right conduct.

A verse from the Quran places value on righteousness as a guarantee for no fear and no grief,

Those who believe (in the Quran), those who follow the Jewish (scriptures), and the Sabians and the Christians,-any who believe in God and the Last Day. and work righteousness, on them shall be no fear, nor shall they grieve.[20]

Verses on God-wariness

The Old Testament

Behold God is my salvation. I will trust and will not be afraid for God the Lord is my strength and song and He is become my salvation.
Isa 12:2

For you have made the Lord who is my refuge even the Most High, your habitation. There shall no evil befall you, neither shall any plague come near your tent.
PSA 91:9-10

And the work of righteousness shall be peace and the effect of righteousness, quietness and confidence forever.
Isa 32:17

Now therefore fear the Lord and serve Him in sincerity and in truth and put away the gods which your fathers served beyond the river and in Egypt and serve you the Lord.
Josh 24:14

The New Testament

Let the peace of God rule in your heart.
Col 3:15

The God of hope fills you with all joy and peace in believing that you may abound in hope.
Rom 15:13

Be perfect, be of good comfort, be of one mind, live in peace and the God of love and peace shall be with you.
II Cor 13:11

Whosoever keeps his word, in him verily is the love of God perfected.
John 2:5

Let not your heart be troubled. You believe in God. Believe also in me.
John 14:1

Peace I leave with you, my peace I give unto you, not as the world gives, give I unto you. Let not your heart be troubled, neither let it be afraid.
John 14:27

God has not given us the spirit of fear but of power and of love and of a sound mind.
II Tim 1:7

Perfect love casts out fear.
John 4:18

The Quran

O you Children of Adam! Whenever there comes to you Messengers from among you, rehearsing My Signs unto you, those who are righteous and mend (their lives), on them shall be no fear nor shall they grieve.
7:35

Verily those who say, 'Our Lord is God," and remain firm (on that path), on them shall be no fear nor shall they grieve.
46:13

Nay, whoever submits his whole self to God and is a doer of good, He will get his reward with his Lord on such shall be no fear nor shall they grieve.
2:112

Those who believe and do deeds of righteousness and establish regular prayers and regular charity will have their reward with their Lord. On them shall be no fear nor shall they grieve.
2:277

SAYINGS ON GOD-WARINESS

The thing which will make the majority of people enter the paradise is fear of God and good manners.

He who helps his fellow-creature in the hour of need, and he who helps the oppressed, him will God help in the day of resurrection.

Who is the most favored of God? He from whom the greatest good comes to His creatures.

Traditions of Prophet Muhammad

Fear God; for He hears all you say, and knows all your thoughts.

Ali ibn Abi Talib

Through self-knowledge a man goes beyond grief.

He who knows the joy of Brahman, which words cannot express and the mind cannot reach, is free from fear.

Upanishad

They live in wisdom who see themselves in all and all in them, who have renounced every selfish desire and sense craving tormenting the heart.

Neither agitated by grief nor hankering after pleasure, they live free from lust and fear and anger. Established in meditation, they are truly wise. Fettered no more by selfish attachments, they are neither elated by good fortune nor depressed by bad. Such are the seers.

He whose mind is not troubled in sorrow and has no desire in pleasure, his passion, fear, and anger departed, he is called a steady-minded sage.

The Bhagavad Gita

Human grief, anxiety and pain come from impure desires.

Buddha

CHAPTER 6
COMMANDMENTS:
YOU SHALL NOT . . .

Satan-Immorality
Anger-Hatred-Pride
Worldly Wealth-Greed
Usury
Hypocrisy
Backbiting
Adultery
Intoxication
Falsehood
(lying, cheating,
stealing, injustice)

CHAPTER 6
COMMANDMENTS:
YOU SHALL NOT . . .

It is an imperative part of the divine message to command human beings not to walk in the valleys of darkness under the influence of evil forces. They have been warned repeatedly through God's messengers in the languages of their respective nations about the prohibited thoughts, plans, and their implications. In light of the verses from the Quran A. Yusuf Ali has mentioned categories of the interdictions from Almighty God in His authoritative manner.

> The forbidden things are described in four categories: (1) what is shameful or unbecoming; the sort of things which have also legal and social sanction, not of a local but of a universal kind; they may be called offenses against society; (2) sins against self and trespasses or excesses of every sort; these are against truth and reason; here would come in discipline, failure in doing intangible duties not clearly defined by law; selfishness or self-aggrandizement, which may be condoned by custom and not punished by law, etc.; (3) erecting fetishes or false gods; this is treason against the true God; (4) corrupting religion by debasing superstitions, etc.[1]

SATAN-IMMORALITY

At the dawn of creation of man, satan had declared his jealousy and enmity with the human. He had vowed to infuse doubts in the minds of the human beings whenever they would progress towards faith in One God. He had challenged to frustrate the human ambition towards the straight way, from all sides and with possible means and manners. God, in His wisdom and as part of His grand scheme for humanity, had granted this satan a reprieve in his strategy until the Final Day.

It is astonishing to think that satan has put forth an adulterated and depressing alternative to a faith which is meant to purify the mind and elevate the soul. For every act that is beneficial and upright for the humans, satan has fabricated an attractive and enchanting alternative that is harmful in its effects and misleading in its direction. Satanic is thus the label for all the primordial opposing agents to human well-being. It is the complex of all those forces that design, shape and wrap in alluring garment the behavior that is opposite to morality. Satan, with his full force tries to stumble persons on the path of righteousness. The first impious plan with course of action, and a conspiracy, is to use human intelligence and create doubts in a faith about unseen and unperceived God, in the worthiness of His commandments, in the rationality of His will, in the judicious consequences of virtuous deeds and in the efficacy of submission before a Power, inconceivable in human mind and human senses.

The second plank of the wicked and destructive plan is to use ornaments of passion, lewd, and sensual pleasures, fortified with greed, selfishness, pride, worldly wealth and immorality. The third wave of attack is to broadcast seeds of hatred on the souls for other human beings, thus, providing all sorts of evil nourishments through various excuses based on malignant reasonings for creating differences to wage wars, bloodshed, and destruction of the human society. Under these circumstances and conditions of confrontation between right and wrong, God's commandment is as clear as the rising sun.

God Almighty, in His mercy toward humanity, has identified these harmful acts through His revelations and through the exhortations of His appointed messengers. Just as there are the glad- tidings of the beneficial effects of the virtuous deeds, there are warnings against the ill effects of the evil behavior in this world and in the hereafter. To diligently pursue what is right and to be mindful, and ever so vigilant against what is wrong is the ultimate essence of piety and the state of extreme caution in the straight way.

The categories of unaccepted behavior are the following: ridiculing the divine guidance, mischief against the blessed messengers, arrogance, self-worship and self- indulgence, greed and avarice, hoarding of wealth, niggardliness, gluttony and excesses, back- biting, false allegations and rumor mongering, theft and violation of others' rights, unlawful profiteering, perjury and covering of the truth, mischief and malice, lewdness, debauchery and unlawful sexuality.

Histories of human societies testify to the divinely revealed assertion that at the roots of their downfall and decay lies the confusion between the beneficial and the harmful, the lawful and the unlawful, the right and the wrong (forbidden.) Creation of this confusion at the boundaries of these opposites, the truth and falsehood, is the strategic core of satanic persistence against the human being. And it is precisely to maintain the clarity and the fidelity of such boundaries that the divine guidance has been universal.

Satan comes with many faces and forms and has tremendous assortments of tools and weapons in his arsenal to betray humans. The most effective instruments of attack is induction in human minds that he/she is superior to others based on color, creed, gender, physical power, physical appearance, intellectual functioning, inheritance, nationality, destructive power, manipulative power, and even self conception, self deception of piety which is in fact created by humans through self assumed superiority in one's faith and sect. Satan keeps whispering in their ears based on one or combinations of more than one of the above mentioned factors and caters ample excuses to feel vain-glory. Thus seeds of hatred are embedded in soul with false pride and pretension to grow various forms of embitterment towards other human beings. Satan's biggest enjoyment is winning warfare against those who struggle and strive to attain piety through superfluous means and rituals of worship. Human beings, under satanic influence, feel superiority and false pride in self exaltation and self imposed reverence.

The essence of the logic in the universal commandments by God for the humans is that these laws harness the animality and reveal a glorious life in control and command of desires, passions and the world of senses. The obedience to these commandments guarantees and secures progressive ascension to eternal life, free of venomous stings of immorality and mortality.

A human society cannot prosper or even survive when the moral fabric is rotten and shredded. A feeling of insecurity and gloom prevails in every recognized aspect of human life. Even though pleasures, embodied in falsehood, are ruling the human desires. How can there be contentment, happiness and blessings when members of that society lie, steal, cheat, and commit murders. How can respectability, honor and nobility thrive if treachery, adultery and fornication rule under the disguise of personal freedom and liberty of choice in lifestyles. When infidelity and immorality has entered in the inner chambers and corridors of one's home; when peace, happiness and trust have been strangled by the invasion of immorality; a structure is shattered and innocent children's happiness and their future are buried under broken homes and demolished morality. Imagine when the wickedness ridicules the divine message and immorality is accepted and approved under the false pretext of human rights, choice and liberty.

The objections, abhorrence, rejection and condemnations of immorality are germane in the most primitive state of human society. The authorization of crime has never been accepted by the societal code of any society in the recorded history. It would have been totally impossible for humans to live together, love and trust each other in which criminals have licenses to practice. Immorality, disrespect and disregard to standard ethics had led to annihilation of civilization. History believed and testified that the only way to regenerate the society is through orderly social life ornamented with sincerity in personal and public conduct crowned with morality. Gentleman was defined not as a person of noble birth, but as dressed in shinning garb of morality, guided by benevolent rules of conduct and piety.

God has designed and arranged this universe in a way that immorality cannot breathe and breed in it in the long run. Civilizations who had been destroyed and mentioned in the dark chapters of human history met their fatal fates through this plague of wickedness.

VERSES ON SATAN/IMMORALITY

THE OLD TESTAMENT

You shall have no other gods before Me. You shall not make a graven image nor any manner of likeness of anything that is in the heaven above or that is in the earth beneath or that is in the water under the earth. You shall not take the name of the Lord your God in vain for the Lord will not hold him guiltless that takes His name in vain. You shall not commit murder. You shall not commit adultery. You shall not steal. You shall not bear false witness against your neighbor. You shall not covet your neighbor's house. You shall not covet your neighbor's wife nor his manservant nor his maid-servant nor his ox nor his ass nor anything that is your neighbors.
Ex 20:3, 4, 7, 13, 14

THE NEW TESTAMENT

For the commandments: you shall not commit adultery, you shall not murder, you shall not steal, you shall not bear false witness, you shall not cov et and if there is any other commandment, are all summed up in this saying, namely: Love your neighbor as yourself.
Rom 13:9

From within, out of the heart of people proceed evil thoughts, adulteries, fornication, murders, thefts, covetousness, wickedness, deceit, lasciviousness and the evil eye, blasphemy, pride, foolishness: all these evil things come from within and defile the person.
Mark 7:21-23

Let all bitterness and wrath and anger and clamor and evil speaking be put away from you with all malice.
Eph 4:31

Let us not love in word, neither in tongue, but in deed and in truth.
John 3:18

THE QURAN

Take not with God another object of worship or you will sit in disgrace and destitution.\
17:22

Say, "The things that my Lord has indeed forbidden are: shameful deeds, whether open or sec ret, sins and trespasses against truth or reason; assigning of partners to God for which He has given no authority and saying things about God of which you have no knowledge.
7:33

O you that believe! Betray not the trust of God and the Messenger nor misappropriate knowingly things entrusted to you.
8:27

O you who believe! Why say you that which you do not know? Grievously odious is it in the sight of God that you say that which you do not know.
61:2-3

VERSES ON SATAN/IMMORALITY

THE OLD TESTAMENT

You shall not oppress your neighbor nor rob him. The wages of a hired servant shall not abide with you all night until the morning. You shall not curse the deaf nor put a stumbling-block before the blind, but you shall fear your God. I am the Lord. You shall do not unrighteousness in judgment. You shall not respect the person of the poor nor favor the person of the mighty, but in righteousness shall you judge your neighbor. You shall not go up and own as a talebearer among your people. Neither shall you stand idly by the blood of your neighbor. I am the Lord. You shall not hate your brother in your heart. You shall surely rebuke your neighbor and not bear sin because of him. You shall not take vengeance nor bear any grudge against the children of your people, but you shall love your neighbor as yourself. I am the Lord.
Lev 19:13-18

You shall not lie with mankind as with womankind. It is an abomination.
Lev 18:22

You shall not follow a multitude to do evil neither shall you bear witness in a cause to turn aside after a multitude to pervert justice.
Ex 23:2

THE NEW TESTAMENT

Sin is transgression of the law.
John 3:4

He that says, "I know him," and does not keep his commandments is a liar and the truth is not in him.
John 2:4

We should not lust after evil things.
I Cor 10:6

Speak evil of no man.
Tit 3:2

Judge not and you shall not be judged. Condemn not and you shall not be condemned. Forgive and you will be forgiven.
Luke 6:37

Now the works of the flesh are evident which are: adultery, fornication, uncleanliness, lewdness, idolatry, sorcery, hatred, contention, jealousies, outbursts of wrath, selfish ambitions, dissensions, heresies. Envy, murders, drunkenness, revelries and the like of which I tell you beforehand just as I also told you in past time that those who practice such things will not inherit the kingdom of God.
Gal 5:19-21

Let all bitterness, wrath, anger, clamor and evil speaking be put away from you with all malice.
Eph 4:31

THE QURAN

And cover no truth with falsehood nor conceal the truth when you know (what it is).
2:42

For you practice your lusts on people in preference to women. You are indeed a people transgressing beyond bounds.
7:81

O you who believe! Follow not satan's footsteps. If any will follow the footsteps of satan, he will but command what is shameful and wrong. And were it not for the grace and mercy of God on you, not one of you would ever have been pure but God does purify whom He pleases and God is One Who hears and knows (all things).
24:21

Nor take life—which God has made sacred—except for just cause.
17:33

ANGER/HATRED/PRIDE

All feelings of exclusiveness, hatred, anger, abhorrence and repugnance are offshoots of a false self-glorification which is deeply rooted in unscrupulous pride and a superiority complex. It is one of the worst attributes of human beings. This deceptive egotism bruises humble and subservient nature of mankind which, in fact, is crowned with modesty. It demolishes noble virtues. This false pride causes undue anger which, in turn, tarnishes the human soul, which has been destined to bask and enjoy the luxuriant gratification of peace and contentment by the grace of God. Egotistical smugness, especially towards the weak, vulnerable and poor, fires up the fury, hatred and anger of persons in power resulting in tyranny, oppression and injustice.

The glorious chapters are written with blood, sweat and tears of the real pious human beings. They are the true models of submission to His will, the true benefactors of humanity and the light houses in dark dingy voyages. There is not a speck of pride or a grain of abhorrence or any spot of reprehension in their attitude or character. They are, instead, symbols of the Almighty's compassion. In spite of the fact that they receive guidance and support from the divine power, they beg, cry, weep, pray and seek His forgiveness and His mercy in every step and in every moment of their lives is fulfilling their assigned missions. Anger, pride and hatred strangle wisdom, a prize to human beings, and turn the humane feelings and noble actions into insensitivity, brutality, and savageness. Pride, anger, and hatred are condemned in the revelations.

VERSES ON ANGER/HATRED/PRIDE

THE OLD TESTAMENT

Cease from anger and forsake wrath. Fret not yourself. It tends only to evil-doing.
PSA 37:8

He that is slow to anger is of great understanding, but he who is hasty of spirit exalts folly.
Prov 14:29

Multiply not exceeding proud talk. Let not arrogance come out of your mouth.
I Sam 2:3

When pride comes, then comes shame but with the lowly is wisdom.
Prov 11:2

Every one that is proud in heart is an abomination to the Lord. My hand upon it! He shall not be unpunished.
Prov 16:5

THE NEW TESTAMENT

Let all bitterness, wrath, anger, clamor and evil speaking be put away from you with all malice.
Eph 4:31

I say through the grace given unto me to every person that is among you, not to think of himself more highly than he ought to think but to think soberly accordingly as God has dealt to every person the measure of faith.]
Rom 12:3

If a person think himself to be something, when he is nothing, he conceives himself. Let us not be of desirous of vainglory.
Gal 5:26

Be of the same mind toward one another. Do not set your mind on high things, but associate with the humble. Do not be wise in your own opinion.
Rom 12:16

THE QURAN

Those who spend (freely), whether in prosperity or in adversity, who restrain anger and pardon (all) people, for God loves those who do good.
3:134

Those who avoid the greater crimes and shameful deeds and when they are angry even then forgive.
42:37

And swell not your cheek (for pride) at people nor walk in insolence through the earth for God loves not any arrogant boaster. And be moderate in your pace and lower your voice for the harshest of sounds without doubt is the braying of the ass.
21:18-19

SAYINGS ON ANGER/HATRED/PRIDE

Verily, anger spoils faith just as aloes spoils honey.

Whoever suppresses his anger, when he has in his power to show it, God will give him a great reward.

That person will not enter paradise who has one atom of pride in his heart.

Be careful of malice because malice consumes the virtues just as fire consumes fuels.

The proud will not enter paradise, nor a violent speaker.

He will not enter hell, who has faith equal to a single grain of mustard seed in his heart; and he will not enter paradise, who has pride, equal to a single grain of mustard seed, in his heart.

Traditions of Prophet Muhammad

Anger is a raging fire. Whoever can subdue his anger, puts out the fire: whoever cannot, gets burnt himself.

Anger is a species of madness, since repentance succeeds to it; or if it does not, it means that the madness is too firmly established.

The worst man is the one who sees himself as the best.

The wicked man thinks no good of any one; for how should he imagine that others have what he lacks himself?

Oh, how can a son of Adam boast, who begins as a germ, and ends as a corpse; who cannot nourish himself, nor escape death.

Ali ibn Abi Talib

Anger leads to a state of delusion; delusion distorts one's memory. Distortion of memory distorts consciousness, and then a man perishes.

When unpleasant things do not perturb him nor pleasures beguile him, when longing, fear, and anger have left, he is a sage of firm mind.

These men, so full of scorn, rely on their ego, on force on

pride, on lust and wrath, and they hate me in their own body and that of others.

Self-important, obstinate, swept away by the pride of wealth, they ostentatiously perform sacrifices without any regard for their purpose. Egotistical, violent, arrogant, lustful, angry, envious of everyone, they abuse my presence within their own bodies and in the bodies of others.

The Bhagavad Gita

One should give up anger; one should abandon pride; one should overcome all fetters. Ills never befall him who clings not to mind and body and is passionless.

Conquer anger by love, conquer evil by good; conquer the stingy one by giving, conquer the liar by truth.

People love their egoistic comfort, which is a love of fame and praise. But fame and praise are like incense that consumes itself and soon disappears. If people chase after honors and public acclaim and leave the way of truth, they are in serious danger and will soon have cause for regret.

Making their deeds the field for their egos, using the working of discrimination of the mind as seed, beclouding the mind by ignorance fertilizing it with the rain of craving desires, irrigating it by the willfulness of egotism, they add the conception of evil, and carry this incarnation of delusion about with them.

Buddha

When one is angry, if one can directly forget his anger and examine the right and wrong according to principle, then right and wrong will be clearly seen and desires will naturally be unable to persist.

I hate those who are impetuous and consider themselves

wise; I hate those who are not modest and consider themselves courageous; I hate those who attack the secrets of others and consider themselves upright.

Confucius

Fools brag of their knowledge, proud, ignorant, dissolving; staggering to and fro, blind and led by the blind.

Upanishad

Nanak, the man puffed up with his own wisdom will get no honor from it in the life to come.

Guru Nanak

WORLDLY WEALTH/GREED

The life of this world has had a magical and seductive hold on human beings. It is a realm of sensory excitation of desires and dreams. Pleasures of the body and excitation of the mind and emotions design the models of behavior. Any delay in their gratification fuels the desire. Wishes are always running ahead of possessions. Most of human energy, including intelligence, creativity and raw power, is aimed at fulfilling those wishes. It has been generally understood and accepted by human beings that those who have power can accumulate riches and those who are rich can influence and even purchase power. To be rich one aims to accumulate things of value, currency of exchange, commodities, land, and labor force. The excessive love for the worldly life, the pursuit of grandiosity and command over others, the indulgence in the self, the thirst for praise, the gluttony for pleasure, and the accumulation of objects and symbols of power are all rooted in the insecurity of the human psyche that emerges with the erosion of faith in the larger scheme of Creation and in Divine guidance. The unquenchable thirst reflects the greed of a person drenched in compounded worldly desires. The more one is fed, the more one wants. There is not much that separates the motivations of an obsessive miser hoarding coins and the empire builder out to conquer the world. The former reveals in his endless fondling of the coins that are of no use to him or anyone else. The latter builds his towers of human skulls and lives in perpetual fear of the palace revolts or rebellions at the fringes of his empire. In the end both have to surrender to death.

What they leave behind is the history of stealing other's property, trampling on other's rights, and a complex web of tyranny. Their descendants either entrench and perpetuate their misery or some invisible force scatters their wealth like the winter winds carries the dead autumn leaves with it. In the end the ruins of those who were obsessed with the love of this world became the lessons for the future generations that here was an ill-fated barren love that produced no fruits. It can be said with certainty that divine guidance, in all times and all places, has warned human beings against the seductive guiles of exclusive attachment to this world. Divine revelations point out the linkage between the increasing desire for worldly wealth and the decreasing respect for the rights of fellow human beings. Through parables and history of past nations it is brought forth repeatedly that those who ignored the timeless hereafter in exclusive favor of the here and now were in the end disappointed. For temporary benefits of this world that seemed permanent to them, they surrendered the permanent felicity of the hereafter that seemed remote and imaginary to them.

The worst enemy of human beings, since they were chosen to receive divine guidance from God on this planet earth, is satan who with all the forces at his command forbids human beings from the required obedience to God. Satan's most effective and destructive tool is to infest the human mind with selfishness. The manifestation of selfishness is most evident in greed for more worldly pleasures and more wealth, than what the rightfully deserving persons possess. This covetous and grasping selfishness converts the peace of mind into bemoaning soul, bereaved of moral attributes.

In the light of verses from the Holy Quran A. Yusuf Ali has mentioned the harmful effects of selfishness, hoarding, and greed for worldly wealth.

> True knowledge is with God alone. We are not to dispute on matters of conjecture, but to rely on the Truth that comes from God. As in the parable: The man who piles up wealth and is puffed up with this world's goods, despising those otherwise endowed, will come to an evil end, for his hopes were not built on God.[2]

> Many of the attractive vanities of this world are but nets set by the evil one to deceive the human being. The only thing real and lasting is the good life lived in the Light of God.[3]

> The foolish and the wicked set great store by the
> pleasures of this world. In their pride they think they
> have all knowledge. In the fullness of knowledge they
> will see how wrong they were. Meanwhile those who
> have received the light should not for a single moment
> wonder at the apparent prosperity of the ungodly in
> this world. They should leave them alone, confident in
> the goodness and justice of God.[4]

> The true test of progress in spiritual life is to be
> measured by other things than material wealth and
> influence. What we have to ask ourselves is: Are we
> the least bit nearer to God?[5]

Here worldy wealth is defined as selfishness, exploitation
and greed laced with insensitivity towards the needs of our fellow human beings. Universal spirituality has disapproved of
the accumulation of wealth in a few hands acquiring it by
unfair means and usurping the rights of others. Otherwise, conceptual reality and rationality in the divine religion demands
acquiring knowledge for the advancement in science and technology for the benefit and welfare of the entire human race. It
promotes marshalling natural resources and employing God-
given knowledge to launch business enterprises and develop
healthy economic structures based on honesty, fairness and
generosity, an expression of gratitude to the True Sustainer and
Cherisher through altruism.

Every messenger of God has condemned selfishness, greed,
and the accumulation of worldly wealth. The quotations from
the Old and New Testaments, the Quran, Traditions, and other
sources testify the devastations caused by these forbidden greed
in the human society.

VERSES ON WORLDLY WEALTH/GREED

THE OLD TESTAMENT

For we are but of yesterday and know nothing because our days upon earth are a shadow.
Job 8:9

A faithful man shall abound with blessings but he that makes haste to be rich shall not be unpunished. He that has an evil eye hastens after riches and know not that what shall come upon him.
Prov 28:20, 22

When goods increase, they are increased that eat them and what advantage is there to the owner thereof, saying the beholding of them with his eyes?
Eccl 5:10

Yes, the dogs are greedy. They know not when they have enough.
Isa 56:11a

He that trusts in his riches shall fall but the righteous shall flourish as foliage.
Prov 11:28

Better is a little with righteousness than great revenues with injustice.
Prov 16:8

THE NEW TESTAMENT

Friendship of the world is enmity with God.
Jas 4:4

The cares of this world and the deceitfulness of riches and the lusts of other things entering in, choke the word and it becomes unfruitful.
Mark 4:19

And the world is passing away and the lust of it but he who does the will of God abides forever.
John 2:17

Your gold and silver are corroded and their corrosion will be a witness against you and will eat your flesh like fire. You have heaped up treasure in the last days.
Jas 5:3

Then Jesus said to His disciples, "Assuredly I say to you that it is hard for a rich man to enter the kingdom of heaven. And again I say to you, it is easier for a camel to go through the eye of a needle than for a rich man to enter the kingdom of God."
Matt 19:23-24

What is a man profited if he shall gain the whole world and lose his own soul?
Matt 16:26

The love of money is the root of all evil.
I Tim 6:10

THE QURAN

Know you that the life of this world is but play and amusement, pomp and mutual boasting and multiplying (in rivalry) among yourselves, riches and children.
57:20a

Those who love the life of this world more than the hereafter, who hinder (people) from the path of God and seek therein something crooked, they are astray by a long distance.
14:3

The life of this world is alluring to those who reject faith and they scoff at those who believe but the righteous will be above them on the day of resurrection for God bestows His abundance without measure on whom He will.
2:212

Fair in the eyes of men is the love of things they covet: heaped-up hoards of gold and silver, horses branded (for blood and excellence) and (wealth of) cattle and well-tilled land. Such are the possessions of this world's life but in nearness to God is the best of the goals (to return to).
3:14

USURY

A human being who is bounded in the shackles of greed is insensitive to the needs and sufferings of others. This malice of exploitation of others' weaknesses is the driving force behind usury. The greed and self-worship in human dealings have extinguished the spark of divine light in the human soul. In the light of verses from the Quran A. Yusuf Ali has described usury, (*riba* in Arabic):

> *Riba* is any increase sought through illegal means, such as usury, bribery, profiteering, fraudulent trading, etc. All unlawful grasping of wealth at other people's expense is condemned. Economic selfishness and many kinds of sharp practices, individual, national, and international, come under this ban. The principle is that any profit which we should seek should be through our own exertions and at our own expense, not through exploiting other people or at their expense, however we may wrap up the process in the spacious phraseology of high finance or city jargon. But we are asked to go beyond this negative precept of avoiding what is wrong. We should show our active love for our neighbors by spending of our own substance or resources or the utilization of our own talents and opportunities in the service of those who need them. Then our reward or recompense will not be merely what we deserve. It will be multiplied to many times more than our strict account.[6]

The messengers of God have condemned usury in the Old and New Testaments and the Quran.

VERSES ON USURY

THE OLD TESTAMENT

You shall not lend upon interest to your brother, interest of money, interest of victuals, interest of anything that is lent upon interest.
Deut 23:20

And if your brother be waxen poor, and his means fall with you, then you shall uphold him as a stranger and a settler shall he live with you. Take you no interest of him or increase but fear your God that your brother may live with you. You shall not give him your money upon interest nor give him your victuals of increase.
Lev 25:35-37

THE NEW TESTAMENT

Give to him that ask you and from him that would borrow of you turn not away.
Matt 5:42

If he lend to them of whom you hope to receive what thank have you?
Luke 6:34

THE QURAN

O you who believe! Devour not usury doubled and multiplied but fear God that you may prosper.
3:130

God will deprive usury of all blessing but will give increase for deeds of charity for He loves not creatures ungrateful and wicked.
2:275-276

SAYINGS ON USURY

The taker of usury and the giver of it, and the writer of its papers and the witness to it, are equal in crime.

Whoso desires that God should redeem him from the sorrows and travail of the last day, must delay in calling on poor debtors, or forgive the debt in part or whole.

Traditions of Prophet Muhammad

HYPOCRISY

Expression of all the verbal adherence to the divine message while nourishing the evil feelings against that message, exhibit, defend and harbor the animosities against the divinity. This is the worst and the most dangerous form of human feelings and behavior. Their ways, actions, and deeds are just the opposite of what they profess by mouth. They exhibited hollowness and twisted faith with deceitful mind. God's religion, throughout the span of time in human societies, has called hypocrisy the most dangerous disorder, a malady of the human mind and soul. These fraudulent deceivers are in fact cancerous growths on humanity and thus ultimately demolish the peace and harmony in human society. They are dangerously intelligent and skillfully selfish. They seed facade and mischief in society in the name of peace and conciliation. The shrewdness and intrigues are all directed to harm the cause of God's religion, although they carry a label of believers. Their pretense and double-dealings have harmed the true believers more than the nonbelievers. In the light of verses from the Holy Quran, A. Yusuf Ali has described how to treat them.

> How should hypocrites be treated? To take them into your confidence would of course be foolish. To wage unrelenting war against them may destroy the hope of reforming them and purging them of their hypocrisy. The man of God keeps clear of their wiles, but at the same time does not hesitate to show them the error of their ways, nor to put in a word in reason, to penetrate their hearts and win them back to God.[7]

VERSES ON HYPOCRISY

THE OLD TESTAMENT

This also shall be my salvation that a hypocrite cannot come before him.
Job 13:16

Every way of a man is right in his own eyes but the Lord weighs the hearts.
Prov 21:2

Hear now this, O foolish people, and without understanding that have eyes and see not, that have ears and hear not.
Jer 5:21

THE NEW TESTAMENT

Let love be without hypocrisy. Abhor what is evil. Cling to what is good.
Rom 12:9

No man can serve two masters: for either he will hate the one and love the other or else he will hold to the one and despise the other. You cannot serve God and mammon.
Matt 6:245

You are they which justify yourselves before people but God knows your hearts.
Luke 16:15

They profess that they know God but in works they deny him.
Tit 1:16

They seeing see not and hearing they hear not neither do they understand.
Matt 13:13

THE QURAN

The hypocrites, men and women (have an understanding) with each other. They enjoin evil and forbid what is just and are close with their hands. They have forgotten God so He has forgotten them. Verily the hypocrites are rebellious and perverse.
9:67

The hypocrites—they think they are over-reaching God, but He will over-reach them. When they stand up to pray, they stand without earnestness to be seen by people but little do they hold God in remembrance.
4:142

SAYINGS ON HYPOCRISY

The characteristics of a hypocrite are three : As he speaks, he lies; as he makes a promise, he violates (it); as he is trusted, he acts treacherously.

Two traits cannot unite in a hypocrite; good conduct and knowledge.

Whoever has got two faces in this world will have two

tongues of fire on the Resurrection Day.

The example of a hypocrite is that of a roaming ewe between two flocks. It turns at one time to one, and at another to the other.

Tradition of Prophet Muhammad

Hypocrites robe themselves in lies.

The hypocrite has a sweet tongue, but a bitter heart.

Ali ibn Abi Talib

Hypocritical, proud, and arrogant, living in delusion and clinging to deluded ideas, insatiable in their desires, they pursue their unclean ends. Although burdened with fears that end only with death, they still maintain with complete assurance, "Gratification of lust is the highest that life can offer."

Other qualities, Arjuana, make a person more and more inhuman: hypocrisy, arrogance, conceit, anger, cruelty, ignorance.

The Bhagavad Gita

To preach and not to practice it is to be like a parrot saying a prayer.

Buddha

BACKBITING

One kind of dangerous tool that shreds into pieces the fabric of mutual courtesy and respect amongst human beings is finding faults, being suspicious, and condemning others who are absent as a fun loving exercise in conversations and statements. A. Yusuf Ali in the light of a verse from the Quran has explained it,

> Most kinds of suspicion are baseless and to be avoided, and some are crimes in themselves: for they do cruel injustice to innocent men and women. Spying, or inquiring too curiously into other people's affairs, means either idle curiosity, and is therefore futile, or suspicion carried a stage further, which almost amounts to sin. Backbiting also is a brood of the same genus. It may be either futile but all the same mischievous, or it may be poisoned with malice, in which case it is a sin added to sin. No one would like even to think of such an abomination as eating the flesh of his brother. But when the brother is dead and the flesh is carrion, abomination is added to abomination. In the same way we are asked to refrain from hurting people's feelings when they are present; how much worse is it when we say things, true or false, when they are absent![8]

VERSES ON BACKBITING

THE OLD TESTAMENT

You shall not go up and down as a talebearer among your people neither shall you stand idly by the blood of your neighbor. I am the Lord.
Lev 19:16

And evil doer gives heed to wicked lips and a liar gives ear to a mischievous tongue.
Prov 17:4

THE NEW TESTAMENT

Do violence not to man neither accuse any falsely.
Luke 3:14

Let all bitterness and evil speaking be put away from you with all malice.
Eph 4:31

Speak evil of no man.
Tit 3:2

THE QURAN

O you who believe! Avoid suspicion as much as possible for suspicion in some cases is a sin. And spy not on each other nor speak ill of each other behind their backs. Would any of you like to eat the flesh of his dead brother? Nay, you would abhor it.
49:12

SAYINGS ON BACKBITING

Refrain from seeing and speaking of the vices of mankind, which you know are in yourself.

Backbiting vitiates ablution and fasting.

It is unworthy of a mumin (believer) to injure people's reputations; and it is unworthy to curse any one; and it is unworthy to abuse any one; and it is unworthy of a mumin (believer) to talk vainly.

Traditions of Prophet Muhammad

Beware of backbiting: it sows the seeds of bitterness, and separates you from God and men.

Whoever listens to slander is himself a slanderer.

Ali ibn Abi Talib

If a man looks after the faults of others and is always inclined to be offended, his own passions will grow, and he is far from the destruction of passion.

Buddha

ADULTERY

The misdirected human passions end up in the shameful and immodest alleys of immorality. Sexual feelings, an automatic and natural sentiment, are a vital force, harnessed by a moral code, for the continuation of human progeny. Every religion under divine guidance has fettered the virility of this instinct virtually for the social and moral health of human society. The most shameful affect of this unbounded sensuality is that it drags human beings into a blundering state of unmindfulness of legitimacy and illegitimacy of this pleasureful natural act. Prophet Muhammad said, "Beware of fornication. There is fornication for every part. Fornication with the eyes is a lustful gaze; fornication with the hand is a lustful touch; fornication with the tongue is lustful talk; and fornication with the mind is lustful thought and false fantasy."

VERSES ON ADULTERY

THE OLD TESTAMENT

You shall not commit adultery.
Ex 20:13

He that commits adultery with a woman lacks understanding. He does it that would destroy his own soul.
Prov 6:32

And if a man lie with mankind as with womankind, both of them have committed abomination. They shall surely be put to death. Their blood shall be upon them.
Lev 20:13

THE NEW TESTAMENT

Fornication and all uncleanness, let it not be once named among you.
Eph 5:3

Mortify therefore your members which are upon earth; fornication, uncleanness, inordinate affection, evil concupiscence.
Col 3:5

Likewise also the men, leaving the natural use of the woman, burned in their lust for one another, men with men committing what is shameful and receiving in themselves the penalty of their error which was due.
Rom 1:27

THE QURAN

Nor come near to adultery for it is a shameful deed and an evil opening the road (to other evils).
17:32

Do not come near to shameful sins (illegal sexual intercourse) whether open or secret.
6:151

For you practice your lusts on men in preference to women. You are indeed a people transgressing beyond bounds.
7:81

SAYINGS ON ADULTERY

I swear by God, there is not anything which God so abhors, as adultery.

Modesty and chastity are parts of the faith.
Traditions of Prophet Muhammad

To commit adultery is degradation of the human status. One falls to a level below animals.
Ali ibn Abi Talib

A person whose abode is desire has woman as gods, wor-ships 'Kama:' desire for sexual pleasures.
Upanishad

"There is no God," they say, "no truth, no spiritual law, no moral order. The basis of life is sex; what else can it be?" Holding such distorted views, possessing scant discrimination, they become enemies of the world, causing suffering and destruction.

There are three gates to this self-destructive hell: lust, anger, and greed. Renounce these three. Those who escape from these three gates of darkness, Arjuna, seek what is best and attain life's supreme goal.
The Bhagavad Gita

Rid yourself of your arrogance and your lustfulness, your ingratiating manners and your excessive ambition. These are all detrimental to your person. This is all I have to say to you.
Lao Tzu

How can you indulge in lustful desires? Think of its tran-siency; how can you fall into delusion about it and cherish self-ishness:

Of all the worldly passions, lust is the most intense. All other worldly passions seem to follow in its train.

Lust seems to provide the soil in which other passions flourish. Lust is like a demon that eats up all the good deeds of the world. Lust is a viper hiding in a flower garden; it poisons those who come in search only of beauty. Lust is a vine that climbs a tree and spreads over the branches until the tree is strangled. Lust insinuates its tentacles into human emotions and sucks away the good sense of the mind until the mind withers. Lust is a bait cast by the evil demon that foolish people snap at and are dragged down by into the depths of the evil world.

Buddha

INTOXICATION

The most outstanding, benign and gracious favor of the most benevolent God is showering the human mind with faculties and abilities to think properly, ponder deeply and differentiate judiciously between right and wrong. Human beings are privileged amongst His creation with these vested aptitudes and peculiarities. The divine message is for the benefit and salvation of human beings. As long as they are properly equipped with these abilities to comprehend the difference between right and wrong and can foresee the consequences of their exhibited passions and deeds there is a hope for salvation and ascension. Intoxication of the human mind with drugs, alcohol, or any form of narcotics will shrivel the faculties to differentiate between right and wrong. The use of alcohol and narcotics has caused innumerable miseries, grief, and sorrow in human society. Crime, violence, accidents, and immorality prosper beyond proportion. It is, therefore, forbidden in the revelations.

VERSES ON INTOXICATION

THE OLD TESTAMENT

Harlotry, wine and new wine take away the heart.
Hos 4:11

Wine is a mocker, strong drink is riotous and whosoever reels thereby is not wise.
Prov 20:1

Now therefore beware, I pray you and drink no wine nor strong drink and eat not any unclean thing.
Judg 13:4

Be not among winebibbers, among gluttonous eaters of flesh for the drunkard and the glutton shall come to poverty and drowsiness shall cloth a man with rags.
Prov 23:20, 21

THE NEW TESTAMENT

Be not drunk with wine wherein is excess.
Eph 5:18

Let us walk properly as in the day not in revelry and drunkenness, not in lewdness and lust, not in strife and envy.
Rom 13:13

THE QURAN

They ask you concerning wine and gambling. Say, "In them is great sin and some profit for men but the sin is greater than the profit." They ask you how much they are to spend. Say, "What is beyond your needs." Thus does God make clear to you His signs in order that you may consider.
2:219

SAYINGS ON INTOXICATION

A fornicator when he commits fornication, is not a believer; a thief when he steals, is not a believer; an inebriate when he drinks, is not a believer; a robber when he plunders due to which men raise their looks at him, is not a believer; and none of you when he defrauds, is a believer; so beware, beware!

He is not a good believer (mumin) who commits adultery or gets drunk, who steals, or plunders, or who embezzles; beware, beware.

Traditions of Prophet Muhammad

FALSEHOOD (LYING, CHEATING, STEALING, INJUSTICE)

The multifaceted falsehood in human society is like a cancer strangling the peace, contentment, and love which provide liveliness in a society. The cruel and sinful hands of falsehood cut the roots of virtuous growth. The spiritual development and enlightenment are suffocated with dark and dense smoke of falsehood. The afflictions caused by falsehood are hard to measure with psychological tools. How can one apply standards of measurement to dry, dead, leaves of autumn being turned into pieces and blown away in different directions at the mercy of winter winds. Every known human society in recorded history has condemned falsehood in every shape and form.

PART III
ACTION

CHAPTER 7
CONSEQUENCES

CHAPTER 7
CONSEQUENCES

CONSEQUENCES OF SUBMISSION TO HIS WILL

The created purpose of human beings is to achieve a state of obedience and subservience to the One God and no one else. It is to establish and maintain a state of justice, harmony and peace with one's self, one's fellow human beings, and with all other creations, to earn the blessings of Almighty, and ultimately to become worthy of the state of felicity in the hereafter. The prescription for achieving this purpose is to consciously and sincerely embrace the divine guidance and let its commandments become the foundations and the pillars on which the superstructure of personality and the society is constructed.

Divine guidance instills in humans reasoning, governing the sublime logic that what is useful to them is also beneficial for other members of the mankind. It is a illuminated face of justice. It is an attestation of human honor. It is a certification of nobility in character. It is a guarantee for liveliness of the human spirit and contentment of the soul. It happens with God's blessings.

Guidance that shows no beneficial results for the human condition, individual or societal, cannot possibly be the guidance from the Creator of humankind. It is a misnomer. And the true guidance from Him, followed with all the protocol of subservience must lead to benefits here, and salvation and felicity in the hereafter.

The contrast is evident like day and night between those who spend every moment of their lives in accordance with God's will, obedience of His laws, and are thus citizens of God's kingdom and those who are rebellious against His sovereignty. They are never alike. The righteous ones can see through their enlightened souls and the impious ones are blind in spite of normal eyesights.

A. Yusuf Ali has deduced the meaning of verses from the Quran,

> (1) The evil ones are not in God's sight like the righteous ones; neither in life nor in death are they equal; in life the righteous are guided by God and receive His Grace, and after death His Mercy, while the others reject His Grace and after death receive condemnation. (2) Neither are the two the same in this life and in the after life if the wicked flourish here, they will be condemned in the hereafter; if the good are in suffering or sorrow here, they will receive comfort and consolation in the hereafter. (3) The real life of the righteous—for they have received spiritual life—is not like the nominal life of the wicked, which is really death; nor is the physical death of the righteous, which will bring them into eternal life, like the terrible death of the wicked, which will bring them to eternal misery.[1]

The relationship between cause and effect is certain, clear and logical. Human beings stand or fall, live or die, by their record of deeds. But there is always a bright hope in the doctrine of grace. Human beings have every chance to repent and beg for mercy of the Most Merciful and the Most Compassionate God and later on can improve honestly and sincerely his/her record with righteous deeds.

In the light of verses from the Quran A. Yusuf Ali has mentioned the consequences of striving in Almighty God's service,

Those who strive and suffer in God's cause are

promised (1) a mercy specially from Himself, (2) His
own good pleasure, (3) gardens of perpetual delight.
(4) the supreme reward, God's own presence or nearness. These are in gradation: (1) is a special mercy,
higher than flows out to all creatures; (2) is a consciousness of God's good pleasure, which raises the
souls above itself; (3) is that state of permanent spiritual assurance, which is typified by gardens of perpetual delight, and (4) is the final bliss, which is the
Presence of God Himself, or, in Sufi language didar-i-
llahi, the sight of God Himself.[2]

Prophet Muhammad explained cause-effect, "Verily your
deeds will be brought back to you, as if you yourself were the
creator of your own punishment."

Studying the history of guidance and its manifestations in
human endeavor, one wonders about the high levels of human
determination and patience. How do these sincere believers
confront the doubts that awaken inside and the temptations
that attack from the outside? How they defeated the fears, anxieties and insecurities of this life and attained a state of life
beyond the constraints of mortality? The revelations of God
have amply pointed towards answers to such questions. In this
sphere the relationship between the human actions and their
consequences have been clearly established, as mentioned pre-
viously. The believers' hearts beat with the guidance and their
minds are illuminated by its brilliance. They have been embell-
ished by His commandments. Their speech has become so close
to their actions that their very presence in a community is an
eloquent sermon. They are steadfast and perseverant in their
commitments to the Creator. They become worthy of receiving
the divine greetings. To them come the glad-tidings of the felicity from the Almighty. It is they who have been identified as the
successful. The angels descend on their souls and minds. Satan
has become permanently disheartened from them. They have
been declared as the trustees of the apostles and the companions of the holy messengers. In every age and in every settle-
ment they are the living proof of the possibility and reality of
the archetypal servants: the believing, obeying, and diligent
servants of One God. They ultimately establish, in humanly

demonstrable and acceptable terms, the relationship between guidance and its beneficent value to human condition.

Honor, reverence and recognition in the sight of God is not due to race, social status, amount of wealth or verbal profession of certain faith, but only to righteous conduct, pious attitude, sincere efforts in His cause, love and sacrifice.

The following qualities of servants of God are further described by A. Yusuf Ali in the light of verses from the Quran.

> The higher and more permanent gifts which come from God's Presence are for those who truly worship and serve God. These are described by nine of their characteristics: viz. (1) they have faith: and it follows that (2) they trust in God, instead of running after false standards or values: (3) they eschew the more serious offenses against God;s Law, and of course keep clear of any offenses against sex ("shameful deeds"); (4) while knowing that they are not themselves perfect, they are ready to forgive others, even though they are sorely tried with anger and provocation; (5) They are ready at all times to harken to God's Signs, or to listen to the admonitions of men of God, and to follow the true path, as they understand it; (6) they keep personal contact with God, by habits of prayer and praise: (7) their conduct in life is open and determined by mutual consultation between those who are entitled to a voice, e.g. in private domestic affairs, as between husband and wife, or other responsible members of the household; in affairs of business as between partners or parties interested; and in state affairs, as between rulers and ruled, or as between different departments of administration, to preserve the unity of administration: (8) they do not forget charity, or the help due to their weaker brethren, out of the wealth or gifts or talents or opportunities, which God has provided for themselves; and (9) when other people use them despitefully, they are not cowed down or terrorized into submission and acceptance of evil, but stand up for their rights.[3]

The fact is that one of the highest order of righteous humans is that they are the personification of the truth. They carry a banner of Truth against all wickedness, criminality, viciousness and lustfulness. They stand firm against threats, risks and onslaught of evil forces. The highest form is that they sacrifice their lives and everything by adhering to and maintaining the Truth, without any compromise with evil. They feel and witness His presence by laying their lives in His cause. By doing so they attain the eternal life and live in the holy chambers of the Most sovereign, the Most benevolent and the Most rewarding.

In the Old and New Testaments, the Quran and the Traditions and other resources the rewards and characteristics are described. A few examples are given in the tables.

VERSES ON THE CONSEQUENCES OF SUBMISSION TO GOD'S WILL

THE OLD TESTAMENT	THE NEW TESTAMENT	THE QURAN
For the commandment is a lamp and the teaching is light and reproofs of instruction are the way of life. Prov 6:23	Blessed are they that do His commandments. Rom 22:14	Whosoever works righteousness, man or woman, and has faith. Verily to him will We give a new life, a life that is good and pure and We will bestow on such their reward according to the best of their actions. 16:97
The commandment of the Lord is pure, enlightening the eyes. PSA 19:9	Not the hearer of the law are just before God, but the doers of the law shall be justified. Rom 2:13	
The righteous shall inherit the land and dwell therein forever. PSA 37:29	Whatsoever good things any man does, the same shall he receive of the Lord. Eph 6:8	Those who have faith and do righteous deeds, they are the best of creatures. Their reward is with God: gardens of eternity beneath which rivers flow. They will dwell therein forever. God well pleased with them and they with Him. All this for such as fear their Lord and Cherisher. 98:7-8
Happy are they that are upright in the way who walk in the law of the Lord. Happy are they that keep His testimonies, that seek Him with the whole heart. Yea, they do no unrighteousness. They walk in His ways. PSA 119:1-3	Eye has not seen nor ear heard neither have entered into the heart of the human being, the things which God has prepared for them that love Him. I Cor 2:9	

VERSES ON THE CONSEQUENCES
OF SUBMISSION TO GOD'S WILL

THE OLD TESTAMENT

Sow to yourselves accord-
ing to righteousness, reap
according to mercy, break up
your fallow ground for it is
time to seek the Lord until
He come and cause right-
eousness to rain upon you.
Hos 10:12

If you walk in My statutes
and keep My commandments
and do them, then I will give
your rains in their season
and the land shall yield her
produce and the trees of the
field shall yield their fruit.
Lev 26:3, 4

But the mercy of the Lord
is from everlasting to everlasting upon them that fear
Him and His righteousness
unto children's children. To
such as keep His covenant
and to those that remember
His precepts to do them.
PSA 103:17, 18

He that follows after righteousness and mercy find life,
prosperity and honor.
Prov 21:21

THE NEW TESTAMENT

Blessed are the poor in spirit for theirs is the kingdom of
heaven. Blessed are they that
mourn for they shall be com-
forted. Blessed are the meek
for they shall inherit the
earth. Blessed are they which
do hunger and thirst after
righteousness for they shall
be filled. Blessed are the merciful for they shall obtain
mercy. Blessed are the pure in
heart for they shall see God.
Blessed are the peacemakers
for they shall be called the
children of God. Blessed are
they which are persecuted for
righteousness' sake for theirs
is the kingdom of heaven.
Blessed are you when men
shall revile you and persecute
you and shall say all manner
of evil against you falsely for
My sake.
Matt 5:3-10

The world passes away and
the lust thereof but he that
does the will of God abides
forever.
John 2:17

Godliness with contentment
is great gain.
I Tim 6:6

Whatsoever a man sows,
that shall he reap.
Gal 6:7

To them who by patient continuance in well doing seek
for glory and honor and
immortality, eternal life.
Rom 2:7

THE QURAN

For those who believe and
work righteousness is (every)
blessedness and a beautiful
place of (final) return.
13:29

Then do you remember Me.
I will remember you. Be
grateful to Me and reject not
faith.
2:153

To those who believe and
do deeds of righteousness has
God promised forgiveness
and great reward.
5:10

Those who spend (freely)
whether in prosperity or in
adversity who restrain anger
and pardon (all) men for God
loves those who do good.
3:134

Nay, those that keep their
plighted faith and act
aright—verily God loves
those who act aright.
3:76

SAYINGS ON THE CONSEQUENCES OF SUBMISSION TO GOD'S WILL

If you worship the Compassionate One, provide food and greet all whom you meet, you shall enter paradise in peace.

The generous man is near unto God, near unto paradise, near unto men, and far from hell but the miserly person is far from God, far from paradise, far from men and near hell. Indeed an ignorant person who is generous is dearer to God than a worshipper who is miser.

Verily God created virtues and evil and then explained them. So the person, who resolved to do good but did not, God, the most exalted and hallowed granted him the reward of a full virtue. And if he resolved to do good and acted upon it, God granted him the reward from ten virtues to seven hundred folds (and even) to numberless folds. And if he resolved to do evil but did not perform it God takes it to Him as a complete virtue. And if he resolved to do evil and then did it, God recorded it as a single evil.

It is your own conduct which will lead you to reward or punishment, as if you had been destined therefore.

Traditions of Prophet Muhammad

Blessed is the man who humbles himself before God, whose sources of income are honest, whose intentions are always honorable, whose character is noble, whose habits are sober, who gives away in the name and in the cause of God the wealth which is lying surplus with him, who controls his tongue from vicious and useless talk, who abstains from oppression and tyranny, who cheerfully ad faithfully follows the traditions of the Holy Prophet and who keeps himself away from innovations in religion.

No deed is more profitable than good deeds.

Ali ibn Abi Talib

Sweet are the winds to him who desires for himself moral order; for him the rivers flow sweet.

Rig Veda

According to how one acts, according to how one conducts himself, so does he become. The doer of good becomes good. The doer of evil becomes evil.

'Welcome! Welcome!' cry his pleasant flattering good deeds, as the tongues, emblem of the solar rays, carry him. 'Look upon what we have made for you, look upon this beautiful paradise.'

Upanishads

These who abide in goodness go on high.

From worship comes the rain.

The man of discipline, abundantly endowed with wisdom and sense, solitary and unshakable, controlled, has true harmony. Lumps of earth, rocks, gold, are alike to him.

The divine qualities lead to freedom; the demonic, to bondage. But do not grieve, Arjuna; you were born with divine attributes.

The Bhagavad Ghita

It is in the way of heaven to show no favoritism. It is forever on the side of good man.

Lao Tzu

They who imagine truth in untruth, and see untruth in truth, never arrive at truth, but follow vain desires. They who know truth in truth, and untruth in untruth, arrive at truth and follow true desires.

I bring you great and good news. There is a way from the crushing miseries of this transitory life to real happiness, and it is open to all. But the way is hard, and there is no magical method of making it easy. It means strenuous and constant self-examination; it means renouncing all that you foolishly prize now—your present self, in fact, with all the ignorant crazings and blind urges that make it what it is. No one can tread this path for you, neither god nor man; you must tread it for yourself. So begin now. Be alert, and steadfastly alert. Make the most sustained effort of which you are capable. Let nothing entice you to dally by the wayside— neither self-indulgence, nor the mistaken urge to self-punishment, nor vain metaphysical curiosity, nor the desire for companionship with those not yet ready to enter upon the path. Face uncompromising toward the goal and victory over self—the greatest of all victories, and the key to peace and joy in this life and beyond—will be won.

The virtuous man delights in this world, and he delights in the next; he delights in both. He delights and rejoices, when he sees the purity of his own work.

Buddha

We do not become sinners or saints, by merely saying we are; it is actions that are recorded; according to the seed we sow, is the fruit we reap.

All these lives are judged by their actions. God is True and in His court is truth dispensed; there the elects are acceptable to Him, and by His grace and His mercy honored in His presence. In that court the bad shall be sifted from the good. When we reach His court, O Nanak, we shall know this to be true.

He shall become pure whosoever repeats His Name with devotion, affection and heartfelt love.

Nanak is a servant to those who remain unattached in the world, in whose hearts the one God abides, who live without desires in the midst of desires, and who see and show to others the inaccessible and incomprehensible God.

To abide by Your Will, O Lord is man's best offering to You Who are Eternal. Abiding in Your peace is the reward.

Guru Nanak

THE CONSEQUENCES OF DISOBEDIENCE

One of the greatest gifts of God to human beings is the faculty and the ability to comprehend, distinguish and discriminate between right and wrong. The unfortunate ones, under the influence of lustful desires propagated by satan, reject the righteousness. This worst folly of disobedience must bear the consequences of punishment and doom, irrespective of the color, creed, social status and nationality of the disobedient.

Prophet Moses warned,

Every man shall be put to death for his own sin.
—Deut 24:16—

Prophet Jesus has expressed the consequences of lust,

When lust has conceived, it brings forth sin; and sin, when it is full grown, it brings forth death.
—Jas 1:15—

A. Yusuf Ali, in the light of verses of the Holy Quran, has described this phenomena:

> Man's generic covenant, which flowed from his exercising the option given him, choosing will, forbearance, love, and mercy, made it necessary that breach of it should carry its own punishment. Breach of it is here classed under two heads: those who betray their trust act either as hypocrites or as unbelievers. Hypocrites are those who profess faith but bring not forth the fruits of faith. Unbelievers are those who openly defy faith, and from whom therefore no fruits of faith are to be expected.[4]

If the apparent following of the divine commandments has neither purified the soul, nor enlightened the mind, nor brought the behavior to the service of societal well-being, then one may observe that there is some pollution creeping into intention of faith and the obedience. One may conclude that the nature and purpose of One God's religion has not taken roots in the personality, the piety is an empty act and not a real commitment to the station of obedience. It becomes a misnomer. If the fears and anxieties have increased instead of lessening; if the greed for power and riches still rules the decisions; if sharing ones earnings with the needy is still a painful act; if niggardliness still strangles the tendencies towards charity; if the life is still being governed by the pursuit of the unlawful pleasures; if the mind is still bent upon scheming to cheat others; if tribal, national,ethnic, linguistic chauvinism still comes in the way treating the others justly and with magnanimity; if forgiving others' weaknesses is still very difficult; if exaggerating others' mistakes and rejoicing at others' misfortunes is still an enjoyable pastime... then one may safely conclude that the guidance being followed is some impostrous system, or that the True essence of the Divine guidance has been extracted out and discarded and one is following some lifeless conventions of religious rituals.

One of the outstanding characteristic of sins is that it camouflages itself and traps human senses, dragging them down in dark ditches. 'Satan' relishes mortification, humiliation and degradation of human beings wandering on the condemned paths of immorality. This happens as the inevitable consequence of abandonment or recession of Almighty God's grace, mercy and guidance caused by repeated disobedience to His commandments.

In the light of the verses of the Quran A. Yusuf Ali has described the consequences of evil deeds:

> If we choose evil deliberately and double our guilt by fraud and deception we do not deceive God, but we deceive ourselves. We deprive ourselves of the Grace of God, and are left straying away from the Path. In that condition who can guide us or show us the Way? Our true and right instincts become blunted: our fraud makes us unstable in character: when our fellow men

find out our fraud, any advantages we may have
gained by the fraud are lost: and we become truly dis-
tracted in mind.[5]

The abiding Punishment will be for those who had
willfully and persistently rebelled against God, "transgressing all bounds", and had given themselves up to
the vanities and lusts of this lower life. This punishment will not touch those who had repented and been
forgiven, nor those guilty, through human frailty, of
minor sins, whose deeds will be weighed in the balance against their good deeds.[6]

There has never been a slightest doubt in the minds of
serene, refined and enlightened people that falsehood, disloyal-
ty, dishonesty, moral corruption, deceitfulness, theft, treachery
and murder end up in doom, destruction and annihilation. The
consequences of disobedience to His commandments are mentioned in the Old and New Testaments, the Quran and the
Traditions and in other sources of wisdom.

VERSES ON THE CONSEQUENCES OF DISOBEDIENCE

THE OLD TESTAMENT

But if you will not hearken unto Me and will not do all these commandments, and if you shall reject My statutes and if your soul abhor My ordinances so that you will not do all My commandments but break My covenant, I also will do this unto you: I will appoint terror over you even consumption and fever that shall make the eyes fail and the soul to languish and you shall sow your seed in vain for your enemies shall eat it. And I will set My face against you and you shall be smitten before your enemies. They that hate you shall rule over you and you shall flee when none pursues you. And if you will not yet for these things hearken unto Me, then I will chastise you seven times more for your sins. And I will break the pride of your power. I will make your heaven as iron and your earth as brass. And your strength shall be spent in vain for your land shall not yield her produce neither shall the trees of the land yield fruit. And if you walk contrary to Me and will not hearken unto Me, I will bring seven times more plagues upon you according to your sins.
Lev 26:14-21

THE NEW TESTAMENT

To him that know to do good and do it not to him it is sin.
Jas 4:17

But do you want to know, O foolish person, that faith without works is dead.
Jas 2:20

When lust has conceived, it brings forth sin and sin when it is finished, bring forth death.
Jas 1:15

The wages of sin is death.
Rom 6:23

He that does wrong shall receive for the wrong which he has done and there is no respect of persons.
Col 3:25

For the wrath of God is revealed from heaven against all ungodliness and unrighteousness of people who suppress the truth in unrighteousness.]
Rom 1:18

Neither fornicators nor idolaters nor adulterers nor effeminate nor abusers of themselves with mankind nor thieves nor covetous nor drunkards nor revilers nor extortioners shall inherit the kingdom of God.
I Cor 6:9, 10

THE QURAN

To those who reject Our Signs and treat them with arrogance, no opening will there be of the gates of heaven nor will they enter the garden until the camel can pass through the eye of the needle. Such is Our reward for those in sin.
7:40

But We will certainly give the unbelievers a taste of a severe penalty and We will requite them for the worst of their deeds.
41:27

As for those who divide their religion and break up into sects, you have no part in them in the least. Their affair is with God. He will in the end tell them the truth of all that they did.
6:159

Say, "He has power to send calamities on you from above and below, or to cover you with confusion in party strife giving you a taste of mutual vengeance each from the other." See how We explain the Signs by various (symbols) that they may understand.
6:65

SAYINGS ON THE CONSEQUENCES OF DISOBEDIENCE

He who does not acquire knowledge with the sole intention

of seeking the pleasure of Allah, and does not impart it but for the (partly) gains of the world would not smell the odor of paradise on the day of resurrection.

Neither the deceitful nor the miserly will enter paradise, nor he who misbehaves with one in his possessions.

Traditions of Prophet Muhammad

There is no immunity from His wrath and punishment.

Ali ibn Abi Talib

The ignorant man runs after pleasure, sinks into the entanglements of death.

Upanishads

The evil doer mourns in this world, and he mourns in the next; he mourns in both. He mourns and suffers when he sees the evil result of his own acts.

Whoso in this world destroys life, tells lies, takes what is not given, goes to others' wives, and the man who is addicted to intoxicating drinks, such a one digs up his own root in this very world.

Buddha

There is no crime greater than having too many desires.

There is no disaster greater than not being content.

It is the will of heaven that men should love one another without discrimination, and those who fail to do so will be punished.

Lao Tzu

NOTES

PREFACE
1. Hans Kung, p. 442.
2. This is the gist of quotes in various reports on moral status.

CHAPTER 1: ALMIGHTY GOD
1. *Meaning of the Illustrious Quran*, p. 936
2. *The Spirit of Islam*, p. 150.
3. *The Meaning of the Illustrious Quran*, p. 1087.

CHAPTER 2: CHARACTERISTICS OF THE UNIVERSAL TRUTH
1. *The Spirit of Islam*, p. 175.
2. *Ibid.*, p. 178.
3. *Ibid.*, p. 179.
4. *The Meaning of the Illustrious Quran*, p. 618.
5. *Ibid.*, p. 925.
6. They are different only because human beings under the influence of their arch enemy, satan, have given them different labels for the sake of finding an excuse to hate each other.
7. *The Meaning of the Illustrious Quran*, p. 1295.
8. *Ibid.*, p. 883.

CHAPTER 3: CHARACTERISTICS OF MESSENGERS AND PROPHETS OF GOD
1. *The Meaning of the Illustrious Quran*, p. 833.
2. Matthew 5:17.
3. *The Meaning of the Illustrious Quran*, p. 1001.
4. *Ibid.*, p. 791.
5. Quran 5:113-114.
6. Quran 3:45-48
7. Christmas card published by Carlton Cards, Carlton Card Inc., Dallas TX.
8. *The Spirit of Islam*, p. 1.
9. *Ibid.*, p. 51, 52.

CHAPTER 4: COMMANDMENTS
1. *The Meaning of the Illustrious Quran*, p. 311.
2. *Ibid.*, p. 1235.
3. *Ibid.*, p. 1496.

CHAPTER 5: COMMANDMENTS: YOU SHALL . . .
1. *The Meaning of the Illustrious Quran*, p. 547.

2. *Ibid.*, p. 709.

3. *Ibid.*, p. 1296.

4. *Ibid.*, p. 901.

5. *Ibid.*, p. 226.

6. *Ibid.*, p. 84.

7. *Ibid.*, p. 107.

8. *Ibid.*, p. 1560.

9. *The Spirit of Islam*, pp. 54-55.

10. *The Meaning of the Illustrious Quran*, p. 862.

11. *Ibid.*, p. 75.

12. The Quran 4:92; 5:92.

13. I King 21:27.

14. II Sam 12:16.

15. Vol. 2, p. 565.

16. *Ibid.*

17. PSA 31:19.

18. Prov 13:14.

19. The Quran 6:48.

20. The Quran 5:72.

CHAPTER 6: COMMANDMENTS: YOU SHALL NOT . . .

1. *The Meaning of the Illustrious Quran*, p. 348.

2. *Ibid.*, p. 736.

3. *Ibid.*, p. 1504.

4. *Ibid.*, p. 637.

5. *Ibid.*, p. 1145.

6. *Ibid.*, p. 1062.

7. *Ibid.*, p. 199.

8. *Ibid.*, p. 1406.

CHAPTER 7: CONSEQUENCES

1. *The Meaning of the Illustrious Quran*, p. 1360.

2. *Ibid.*, p. 444.

3. *Ibid.*, p. 1316.

4. *Ibid.*, p. 1131.

5. *Ibid.*, p. 226.

6. *Ibid.*, p. 1684.

GLOSSARY

Ahadith: the Traditions of Prophet Muhammad.

Ali ibn Abu Talib: The first and the most devoted disciple of Prophet
Muhammad was born in 610 A.D. in Mecca, Arabia. His
titles were 'Murtaza' (the chosen one), 'Amir-ul-Momineen' (the
leader of the pious and God-fearing persons). He earned these
titles through his unshakable faith and glorious deeds. His piety,
his love of One God, his sincerity and fortitude in following the
religion were of such high order that none could aspire to reach
him. Prophet Muhammad had named him the gateway of
knowledge and wisdom. (The above excerpt is taken from *Nahjul
Balagha*, trs. by Syed Mohammed Askari Jafery, published by
Khorasan Islamic Center, Karachi , Pakistan, 1971. p. 7-11.)

In Hadith number 5916 of *'Sahih Muslim'* by Imam Muslim,
vol. IV p. 1285, rendered into English by Abul Hamid Siddiqui,
published by Kitab Bhavan, New Delhi, India 10th ed., 1994, Holy
Prophet Muhammad said to Ali, "Aren't you satisfied with being
unto me what Aaron was unto Moses?"

Arjuna: A prince from Aryan Dynasty and an important figure in
Indian epic, Mahabharata, was Lord Krishna's beloved disciple
and friend, commanding on a chariot, an army fighting the evil
force.

Asat: Untruth; anything unreal, untrue, or lacking in goodness.

Atman: The soul enlightened by 'Brahman.

Bhagavad Gita: It is a compilation of sermons by Lord Krishna to
Arjuna in a battle between 'Right' and 'Wrong', raging over
eighteen days, which took place at Kurukshetra in northern India
(between 1000 and 700 B.C.). The climatic battle of the
Mahabharata is the most respected epic in Indian literature.
Eknath Easwaran said in the introduction of *The Bhagavad Gita*,
1985. "Gita distills the loftiest truth of India's ancient wisdom
into simple, memorable poetry that haunts the mind and informs
the affairs of every-day life." (p. 2)

The quotations from the *Bhagavad Gita* which are attested by
Old and New Testaments, and the Quran are mentioned in this
book under pertinent topics.

Brahman: Brahman is the Supreme Reality, the Ultimate Reality, the
Absolute Truth, which transcends time, space, and causality and
cannot be comprehended by human thought or rendered in words.
Brahman is without form, sound, touch, smell or taste. His form
is not an object of vision; no one beholds Him with the eye. His

glory prevails on earth, in heaven, in His own seat, the only city of the heart. He looks at all things; knows all things. All things, their nourishment, their names and their forms are from His will. All that He has willed is right." *The Katha Upanishads*

The description of 'Brahman' in the *Upanishads* has been quoted and discussed by Maulana Abu-ul-Kalam Azad (late), a Muslim scholar and education minister of India, in his book: *'Um-ul-Kitab,' Tafsir, Sura-Fatiha* (Holy Quran), published by Islam; Academy, Lahore, Pakistan. (pages 194 to 200).

The gist of the discussion by Maulana Azad is: In the beginning a monotheistic concept, as evident from the description of 'Brahman' was preached amongst the sages and seers in India as a prime religion. Later on the human mind's maneuvering with the Absolute Truth created three hundred and thirty three gods and goddesses as manifestations of One Supreme God and made their idols. Thus monotheism was mingled with polytheism. The elites in religious groups understood the monotheists concept but they explained this to the commoners as a system of competing mythological deities with abstract human and animal forms under the authority of One Absolute Sovereign.

In this book I have quoted from the *Upanishads* exclusively in relation to the One Supreme Reality, the "Brahman," if that is the Almighty One God, the Absolute Truth.

Buddha: The enlightened one. See Lord Buddha.

Dharma: Law, duty; the universal law which holds all life together in unity.

God: The word 'Eloha, and its plural, 'Elohim, are used in the Old and New Testaments (the Scriptures) for the God. The same words 'Elah, Ilah are mentioned in the Quran (Divine Revelations) as 'Allah.' He (Yhwh, God, most High, Creator of heaven and earth) has ninety-nine names reflecting His attributes. There is a tremendous commonality between Hebrew and Arabic names of the One God. His attributes are not separate from Him. He can not be described. "He is what He is."

Guru: is a highly reverend preacher guiding his followers and inculcating in them the universality of the divine message.

Guru Nanak: The first 'Guru' of the Sikhs, a monotheistic religion, was born at Talwandi (Nankana Sahib) near Lahore, India (now in Pakistan) on April 15, 1469. In his early life he was influenced by reformers of the 'Hindu Bhakti' school and by Muslim saints. He served humanity as a devotee and faithful disciple of Almighty

One God. His praise of Almighty God and his preachings coincide with mystic interpretations of monotheistic religions. He emphasized observance of five things i) worship and singing praises of One God ii) charity towards all iii) purification of body and soul iv) service of mankind and obedience to God v) constant recitation of His Name (attributes) and offering prayers to God for His grace and deliverance. The morning prayer opens with basic creed of Sikhism, "There is only One God."

Dr. Zakir Hussein, ex-president of India paying tribute to 'Guru Nanak', the founder of Sikh Religion, said, "He was an apostle of peace, unity, love and brotherhood of man and who was admired and respected for his universal humanism by followers of all faith."

The above quotation is from the foreword by Dr . Zakir Hussein in the book *Guru Nanak, His Life, Time and Teachings*, published by Guru Nanak Foundation, New Delhi, India, 1969. The preceding excerpt is also taken from the same book (p. 35-38).

Hadith: Sayings of Prophet Muhammad, messenger of Almighty God in Arabia.

Hazrat: The most reverend person.

Holy: preceding the names of His messengers and prophets does not attribute divine characteristics to them. It only denotes that they are free of carnal sins and have demonstrated the highest level of piety and perfection in morality as models for the human race.

Imam: The highest form of faith in Almighty One God.

Injeel: The divine revelation from One God to Prophet Jesus.

Islam: Peace by total submission to Almighty God's Will, commandments.

Jen: Humanity; human-heartedness; true manhood; stressing the relationship between man and his fellow men with love, benevolence, kindness and charity. Jen is the essence of Confucius' ethical teachings.

Kama: Selfish desire; greed; sexual desire, sometimes personified as Kamadeva.

Karma: [from kri "to do"] Action; former actions which will lead to certain results in a cause-and-effect relationship.

Lao Tzu: A philosopher, preacher and social reformer was born around half a century B.C. in Li Village of Hu Hsien in the state of Ch'u. He cultivated the way of virtue and his teachings aimed at self-effacement. He preached mysticism and said, "Rid yourself of your

arrogance and your lustfulness, your ingratiating manners and
your excessive ambition. These are all detrimental to your person.
It is the will of heaven that men should love one another without
discrimination, and those who fail to do so will be punished."

(The above excerpt has been taken from *Lao Tzu: Tao Te
Ching*, trs. by D.C. Lan, published by Viking Penguin Inc. New
York: U.S.A. 1963, P.8 and 14.)

Lord Buddha: Siddhartha Gautama, a prince, born about 500 B.C. in
the capital city Kapilavistv in a small state at the southern
foothills of the Himalayas, India. He achieved 'enlightenment'; so
he was known as 'Buddha'. It is generally said that Guatama
Buddha was against the concept of God. Maulana Abu-ul-Kalam
Azad in his book, *"Tafsir Sura-Al-Fatiha* (the first *Sura* of the
Quran) published by Islam Academy, Lahore, 1975. p. 201,202)
has quoted professor S. Radhakrishnan from his book, *'Indian
Philosophy'* vol. I page 453. The fact is that during Buddha's time
a vast majority of human beings in India worshiped every
conceivable power by making their statues and calling them gods
and goddesses by various names. Trade-markets flourished
between the guardians of temples of various gods and their
worshippers. It can be argued that the negation of gods by Buddha
may be due to the deplorable condition of worshiping
hundreds of gods and a widespread exploitation of worshippers by
greed of custodians of the temples. In fact, as mentioned by
Professor Radhakrishnan, Buddha helped to democratize the
philosophy of the *Upanishads*. He made the knowledge in the
Upanishads available for the daily needs of mankind. Maulana
Azad further discussed (*ibid*. p. 204, 205) that about a hundred
years after the death of Gautama Buddha, his followers were
divided into two groups 'Hinayana' and 'Mahayana.' The former
confessed that Guatama Buddha was a human being, enlightened
to be a guide and a preacher. But the later proclaimed him as a
god. Some historians believe that up to the time of Emperor
Asoka, in India (268-239 B.C.) the statues of Buddha were not wor
shipped as a god. In fact, his teachings are about morality, elimi
nation of lust, greed and impure desires. To attain salvation one
must purify his/her mind.

This book is not to discuss or grade any religion. Quotations of
Lord Buddha, not as a god but as an enlightened preacher, which
coincide with the teachings in the Scriptures of monotheistic
faiths on moral issues are included in this book.

Lord Krishna: A royal prince of Aryan dynasty is the most reverend seer mentioned in Indian epic and legend, 'Mahabharata," composed some 2,500 years ago, traditionally attributed to the sage Vyasa. Lord Krishna's sermons to Arjuna during eighteen days of the battle between right and wrong are called '*Bhagavad Gita*,' "Song of the Lord." He preached 'cosmic wisdom' to foster and preserve the universal goodness against the forces constantly working to destroy and corrupt it. He said that the divine spark in the living conscience (the spirit) in human beings cannot be extinguished by 'death.' He emphasized renunciation of selfishness in thought, words, and action, a theme that is common to all mystics, West and East alike. The above excerpt is taken from *The Bhagavad Gita*, introduction section, Translated by Eknath Easwaran, published by Nilgiri Press, Petalurna, Ca, 1985.

Master: is a teacher with outstanding qualities and abilities to introduce reforms in the society.

Master Confucius: A social reformer who emphasized moral laws and principles of social order was born in the town of Tsou, in the country of Lu, China, in 551 B.C. Confucius was ennobled with a title K'ung meaning 'master.' He gave a golden rule for healthy interpersonal relationships. He said, "Do not do unto others what you do not want others to do unto you." Morality is shown to have no connection whatsoever with self-interest. If need be, a person has to sacrifice even his/her life in the path of righteousness. Confucius described Absolute truth as indestructible. Being indestructible, it is eternal. Being eternal, it is self-existent. Being self-existent, it is infinite. Being infinite, it is vast and deep. Being vast and deep, it is transcendental and intelligent. It is because it is vast and deep that it contains all existence. It is because it is transcendental and intelligent that it embraces all existence. (page 125)

His quotations which reflect the enlightenment of mind and soul are included in this book. Confucius said, "To repay evil with kindness is the sign of a generous character. To repay kindness with evil is the sign of a criminal."

Muslim: One who establishes peace by surrendering to One God's Will.

Pir: guiding the desirous humans towards morality and spiritual ascension.

Quran: Also written as Koran is a complication of divine revelations to Prophet Muhammad over a period of 22 years. The divine Message of Almighty One God is in the Arabic language, free of pollution from human intervention and maneuvering.

Rig Veda: The collection of classical and poetic literature, dating from 1500-1000 B.C., expressed the religious beliefs of the 'Aryans' who migrated from central Asia to northern India. The antiquity of the Vedas is mentioned in a book, *'The Upanishads'*, by Swami Nikhilananda, vol. I, published by Harper and Brothers, New York, 1949, (p. 7), quoting Ba'l Gangadhar Tilak, who calculated from astronomical data suggested that the Rig-Veda was brought together about five thousand years, B.C.

Sat: The Real; truth; goodness.

Sura: Chapter of the Holy Quran.

Sura Fatiha: The first chapter of the Holy Quran.

Tafsir: Translation with detail commentary, usually of Quranic verses.

Torah: The divine revelation from One God to Prophet Moses as Law of Moses, outlined in the first five books of the Holy Scriptures (Old Testament): Genesis, Exodus, Leviticus, Numbers, and Deuteronomy.

Universality of the Divine Message: The Creator of the universe provides all the essentials to sustain and nurture His creation. Human beings are bestowed with living conscience and thus, they earn a special status of supremacy over the animal world. In addition to their physical needs, they are granted His divine Message for their spiritual needs. Their salvation and benediction in the society depend on this message. Like all the essentials (sun, air, water, elements) for sustenance of life on this planet, the divine Message is also free and is for every one. Thus , evidence of His justice for the human race is overwhelming.

The Holy Quran has testified the Sacred Law and Guiding Light in 'Tora' (Old Testament) and Injeel (New Testament). H. Q. S. V vs. 47,49, 50, 51. It has also been commanded to: Say ye: *"We believe In God, and the revelation given to us, and to Abraham, Ismail, Isaac, Jacob, And the Tribes, and that given to Moses and Jesus, and that given to (all) Prophets from their Lord: We make no distinction between one and another of them: And we bow to God (in Islam)."* 2:136.

Universality of the divine Truth is manifested in unity of the divine Message, assigned to all His messengers, sent to all nations in their respective languages (Q.S. XIV: v. 4) during varying times in history of mankind. The source of the message is One. The messengers are chosen by that One. Human and societal needs are the same. The means, sources and prescription of salvation are the same. The right has never been wrong and the evil can never embrace the right. Therefore, how can there be a difference in the divine Message.

Furthermore, Almighty God has defined the faith of prophet Muhammad and the true believers: *"The Messenger believes in what has been revealed to him from his Lord, as do the people of faith. each one (of them) believe in God, His angels, His books, and His apostles. We make no distinction (they say) between one and another of His apostles."* And they say: *"We hear, and we obey: (we seek) Thy forgiveness, our Lord, and to You is the end of all journeys."* 2:285.

The above verse has established the divine Truth about faith that belief in One God, His angels, His Books and His Messengers (prophets), without discrimination and difference between messengers, is the basic requirement for foundation of the True faith.

God has judged those as non-believers in true sense who try to differentiate between the divine Message of Almighty God and His messengers and who claim that they believe in some messengers and deny others or who plan to follow a midway course on their personal discretion. Q. S. IV , v. 150, 151.

A holy book which claims to authenticate the truth in other scriptures needs justification of its own authenticity. The Holy Quran fulfills this requirement. Almighty God says: *There hath come to you from God a (new) Light and a perspicuous Book.* 5:17.

The above verse establishes the fact that Holy Quran is a divine Message assigned to Prophet Muhammad, like other Holy Scriptures revealed to other holy messengers before him. One out standing attribute of the Holy Quran is a genuine guarantee from Almighty God for its protection from human contamination, manipulation and fabrication.

We have, without doubt, sent down the Message; and We will assuredly guard it (from corruption). 15:9.

Here Almighty God also challenged nonbelievers to compose verses, even few, that match the verses of the Holy Quran, if they have any doubt about its authenticity as the Word of Almighty God. History has witnessed that for the last fourteen hundred years no individual or group has met this challenge.

In light of the above I have used verses of the Holy Quran as criteria to justify universality of the divine Message. Verses from the Holy Scriptures (Old and New Testament) are cited in the text and the tables. Quotations from other sources: *Hadith* (sayings of Prophet Muhammad), Hazrat Ali, the *Upanishad*, the *Bhagavad Gita*, Master Confucius, Mystic Lao Tzu and Lord Buddha on the pertinent topics are also included in this book, provided these quotations convey the same message and establish the fact that His divine Message has been for all mankind throughout the history as a manifestation of His mercy, compassion and justice. His Truth radiates from every direction of the world. *The Truth (comes) from God alone; so be not of those who doubt. 3:60. Of some prophets We have already told you the story; of others we have not and to Moses God spoke directly; messengers who gave good news as well as warning, that mankind, after (the coming) of the prophets, should have no plea against God: for God is Exalted in Power, Wise. 4:164,165*

The apostles of Almighty God were sent to all mankind. No race, nation, tribe or ethnic group can lay the exclusive claim on the divine Message, thus, denying the Almighty God's justice and grace to others. (more details in chapter II).

Upanishads: Several thousand years have passed since the *Upanishads* were first formulated by the sages and seers of Indo-Aryan race in India. The write-up on the 'Brahman' and the 'atman,' of God and the soul, is the fundamental deliberation of the doctrine of the *Upanishads*. The historical meaning of the word is the knowledge which, when acquired from an authentic teacher, cuts the fetters of ignorance and inculcates the humility and respect toward the teacher. There are eighteen *Upanishads*. In this books only those quotations from the *Upanishads*, are cited which can be attested by the Holy Scriptures of monotheistic faith.

Zabur: The Psalms, divine revelations from One God to Prophet David.

SUGGESTED BIBLIOGRAPHY

I acknowledge with gratitude using the following books as resources:

Achtemeier, Paul and Elizabeth. *The Old Testament Roots of Our Faith*. New York: Abingdon Press, 1962.

Ali ibn Abi Talib. *Nahjul Balagha*. Karachi: Lhorasan Islamic Center, 1968.

Ali, Syed A. *The Spirit of Islam*. London: University Paperbacks, 1967.

Al-Suhrawardy, Allama S. A. A. *The Sayings of Muhammad*. New York: Citadel Presss, 1990.

Armstrong, Karen. *A History of God*. New York: Alfred A. Knoff, 1994.

Attar, Farid-ud-din. Tadhkara Tul-Auliya: Memoirs of Saints. Trans.

Azad, Maulana A. *Um-ul-Kitab*. Lahore: Islami Academy, 1975.

Bagavad Gita. Petaluma: Nilgiri Press, 1985.

Bakhtiar, Laleh. *God's Will Be Done*. Chicago: Kazi Publications, Inc., 1993. Vol. I: *Traditional Psychoethics and Personality Paradigm*; Vol. II: *Moral Healer's Handbook: The Psychology of Spiritual Chivalry*; Vol. III: *Moral Healing Through the Most Beautiful Names: The Practice of Spiritual Chivalry*.

Bakhtiar, Laleh. *SUFI Expressions of the Mystic Quest*. London: Thames and Hudson, 1976.

Bennett, William J., Ed. *The Book of Virtue*. New York: Simon and Schuster, 1993.

Berrey, Lester V. *A Treasury of Biblical Quotations*. Garden City: Doubleday and Co., Inc. 1948.

Besant, Annie. *The Spiritual Life*. Wheaton: Quest Books, 1991.

Burtt, E. A. *The Teachings of the Compassionate Buddha*. New York: New American Library, 1982.

Carter, Jimmy and Rosalyn. Everything To Gain Making the Most of the Rest of Your Life . New York: Kandom House, 1987.

Carter, John Ross, Ed. *Of Human Bondage and Divine Grace*. La Salle: Open Court, 1992.

Chai, Chu and Windberg Chai. *The Sacred Books of Confucius*. NW Hyde Park: University Books, 1965.

Eileen, Eyan and Kathleen Egan. Suffering into Joy: What Mother Theresa Teaches About True Joy . Ann Arbor: Servant Publications, 1994.

Ferre, Frederick, Joseph J. Kockelman and John E. Smith, Eds. *The Challenge of Religion*. New York: The Seabury Press, 1982.

Griffiths, Bede. *Universal Wisdom: A Journey Through the*

Sacred Wisdom of the World. London: Fount, Harper, Collins, 1994.

Haider, Syed Iftikhar. *Al-Salat in Quran*. Islamabad: Academy Adbiyate, 1991.

Heschel, Abraham Joshu. *Man Is Not Alone*. New York: The Jewish Publication Society of America,1951.

Holy Bible. The New King James Version. Thomas Nelson, Inc. 1935.

Holy Quran. Trans. by Abdullah Yusuf Ali. Lahore: Sh. Muhammad Ashraf, 1975.

Holy Quran, The Meaning of the, Vols. 1-16. Trans by S. Abul Ala Maududi. Eng by Ch. Muhammad Akabr. Ed by A. A. Kamal. Lahore: Islamic Publications Ltd, 1967.

Holy Scriptures According to the Masoretic Text. Philadelphia: Publication Society of America, 1955.

Iqbal, Sir Muhammad. *The Reconstruction of Religious Thought in Islam*, 4th ed., New Delhi: Kitab Bhavan, 1990.

Johnston, Francis W. *The Voice of the Saints*. Rockford: Tan Books and Publishers, Inc., 1965.

Kant, Immanuel. *Foundations of the Metaphysics of Morals and What is Enlightenment*. Indianapolis: The Liberal Arts Press, Inc., The Bobbs-Merrill Company, Inc., 1959.

Kitagawa, Joseph Ed. *The History of Religions Essays on Problems of Understanding*. Chicago: The University of Chicago Press, 1967.

Kung, Hans. *Christianity and World Religions*. Trans. Peter Heinegg. New York: Orbis Books, 1993.

Kung, Hans. *On Being a Christian*. Trans. Edward Quinn. Garden City: Doubleday and Co. Inc, 1968.

Kyokai, Bukkyo D. *The Teachings of Buddha*. Tokyo: Toppan Printing Co. 1992.

Lings, Martin. *Muhammad*. Rochester: Inner Traditions, International, Ltd., 1983.

Marshall, Peter. *Nature's Web*, London: Simon and Schuster ltd., 1992.

Maxims of Ali. Trans J. A. Chapman. Lahore: Sh. Muhammad Ashraf Publishers, 1971.

Merkle, John C. Ed. Abraham Joshua Heschel. New York: Macmillan Publishing Co., 1985.

Murdoch, Iris. *Metaphysics as a Guide to Morals*. New York: The Penguin Press, 1992.

Muslim, Imam. *Sahih Muslim*. Trans Abdul Hamid Siddiqi. Lahore: Sh. Ahsraf Publications.

Nasr, Seyyid Hossein. *Islamic Life and Thought*. New York: Suny

Press, 1981.

Nasr, Seyyid Hossein. *Man and Nature*. London: University Paperbacks, 1976.

Nasr, Seyyed H. *Sufi Essays*. Albany: SUNY, 1972.

Nikhilananda, Swami. *The Upanishads*. New York: Harpers and Brothers, 1949.

Novak, Philip. *The World's Wisdom: Sacred Texts of the World Religion*. San Fransisco: Harper Collins, 1994.

Pelikan, Jaroslav, Ed., *The World Treasury of Modern Religious Thought*. Boston: Little Brown and Co., 1990.

Principle Upanisads. Trans. and Ed. S. Radhakrishnan. Harpers, Collins, 1994.

Rao, Ramakrishna K.S. *Significance of Prayer in Islam*. Dehli: Idarah-i-Adabiyat-i-Delli, 1965.

Robertson, Ronald and William R., Garrett. *Religion and Global Order*. New York: Paragon House Publishers, 1991.

Schuller, Robert H. *Living Positively One Day at a Time*. Garden Grove: The Cathedral Press, 1991.

Shad Abdur, Rehman. *Do's and Don'ts in Islam*. Lahore: Kazi Publishing Co., 1988.

Siddiqi, Abdul H. and Abdur Rehman Shad. *Selections from the Holy Quran and Ahadith*. Lahore: Kazi Publications, 1985.

Sidwick, Henry. *The Methods of Ethics*, 7 ed., Indianapolis: Hackett Publishing Co.,1981.

Sikh Religion. Detroit: Sikh Missionary Center, 1990.

Singh, Gurmakh NB., Ed. *Guru Nanak: His Life, Times and Teachings*. New Delhi: National Publishing House, 1969.

Singh, Maharaj Sardar Bahadar Jagat. *The Science of the Soul*, 7 ed. Punjab: Radha Soami Sutsang, Beas, 1987.

Smith, Huston. *The World Religions*. San Francisco: Harper, 1991.

Smith, Wilfred Cantwell. *Islam in Modern History*. New Jersey: Princeton University Press,1957.

Tomlinson, Gerald. *Treasury of Religions Quotations*. New Jersey: Prentice Hall, 1991.

Tzu, Lao. *Tao Te Ching*. Trans. D. C. Lan. New York: Viking Penguin Inc., 1963.

Wonders of Life on Earth. New York: Golden Press, 1960.

Yutang, Lin. Trans. *The Wisdom of Confucious*. New York: Random House, 1994.